ROBERT FROST

100 SELECTED POEMS

COLLECTABLE EDITION

DELHI OPEN BOOKS

100 SELECTED POEMS
COLLECTABLE EDITION
by ROBERT FROST

Published by

Delhi Open Books

G/F, 4771/23, Bharat Ram Road, Daryaganj, New Delhi-110002
Ph.: 91-11-42408081
E-mail: delhiopenbooks2016@gmail.com

ISBN: 978-93-90997-21-3

Cover, Typesetting, and Book Design by **ROHIT**

Robert Frost was born in San Francisco, California, to journalist William Prescott Frost, Jr., and Isabelle Moodie.His mother was a Scottish immigrant, and his father descended from Nicholas Frost of Tiverton, Devon, England, who had sailed to New Hampshire in 1634 on the Wolfrana. Frost was a descendant of Samuel Appleton, one of the early settlers of Ipswich, Massachusetts, and Rev. George Phillips, one of the early settlers of Watertown, Massachusetts. Frost's father was a teacher and later an editor of the San Francisco Evening Bulletin (which later merged with The San Francisco Examiner), and an unsuccessful candidate for city tax collector. After his death on May 5, 1885, the family moved across the country to Lawrence, Massachusetts, under the patronage of Robert's grandfather William Frost, Sr., who was an overseer at a New England mill. Frost graduated from Lawrence High School in 1892.Frost's mother joined the Swedenborgian church and had him baptized in it, but he left it as an adult.

Contents

The Road Not Taken

Two roads diverged in a yellow wood,
And sorry I could not travel both
And be one traveler, long I stood
And looked down one as far as I could
To where it bent in the undergrowth;

Then took the other, as just as fair,
And having perhaps the better claim
Because it was grassy and wanted wear,
Though as for that the passing there
Had worn them really about the same,

And both that morning equally lay
In leaves no step had trodden black.
Oh, I kept the first for another day!
Yet knowing how way leads on to way
I doubted if I should ever come back.

I shall be telling this with a sigh
Somewhere ages and ages hence:
Two roads diverged in a wood, and I,
I took the one less traveled by,
And that has made all the difference.

.

Stopping By Woods On A Snowy Evening

Whose woods these are I think I know.
His house is in the village, though;
He will not see me stopping here
To watch his woods fill up with snow.
My little horse must think it queer
To stop without a farmhouse near
Between the woods and frozen lake
The darkest evening of the year.

He gives his harness bells a shake
To ask if there is some mistake.
The only other sound's the sweep
Of easy wind and downy flake.

The woods are lovely, dark and deep,
But I have promises to keep,
And miles to go before I sleep,
And miles to go before I sleep.

Fire And Ice

Some say the world will end in fire,
Some say in ice.
From what I've tasted of desire
I hold with those who favor fire.
But if it had to perish twice,
I think I know enough of hate
To say that for destruction ice
Is also great
And would suffice.

Nothing Gold Can Stay

Nature's first green is gold,
Her hardest hue to hold.
Her early leaf's a flower;
But only so an hour.
Then leaf subsides to leaf,
So Eden sank to grief,
So dawn goes down to day
Nothing gold can stay.

Acquainted With The Night

I have been one acquainted with the night.
I have walked out in rain - and back in rain.
I have outwalked the furthest city light.

I have looked down the saddest city lane.
I have passed by the watchman on his beat
And dropped my eyes, unwilling to explain.
I have stood still and stopped the sound of feet
When far away an interrupted cry
Came over houses from another street,

But not to call me back or say good-bye;
And further still at an unearthly height,
One luminary clock against the sky

Proclaimed the time was neither wrong nor right.
I have been one acquainted with the night.

A Question

A voice said, Look me in the stars
And tell me truly, men of earth,
If all the soul-and-body scars
Were not too much to pay for birth.

A Prayer In Spring

Oh, give us pleasure in the flowers to-day;
And give us not to think so far away
As the uncertain harvest; keep us here
All simply in the springing of the year.

Oh, give us pleasure in the orchard white,
Like nothing else by day, like ghosts by night;
And make us happy in the happy bees,
The swarm dilating round the perfect trees.

And make us happy in the darting bird
That suddenly above the bees is heard,
The meteor that thrusts in with needle bill,
And off a blossom in mid air stands still.

For this is love and nothing else is love,
The which it is reserved for God above
To sanctify to what far ends He will,
But which it only needs that we fulfil.

A Late Walk

When I go up through the mowing field,
The headless aftermath,
Smooth-laid like thatch with the heavy dew,
Half closes the garden path.

And when I come to the garden ground,
The whir of sober birds
Up from the tangle of withered weeds
Is sadder than any words

A tree beside the wall stands bare,
But a leaf that lingered brown,
Disturbed, I doubt not, by my thought,
Comes softly rattling down.

I end not far from my going forth
By picking the faded blue
Of the last remaining aster flower
To carry again to you.

A Minor Bird

I have wished a bird would fly away,
And not sing by my house all day;

Have clapped my hands at him from the door
When it seemed as if I could bear no more.

The fault must partly have been in me.
The bird was not to blame for his key.

And of course there must be something wrong
In wanting to silence any song.

A Soldier

He is that fallen lance that lies as hurled,
That lies unlifted now, come dew, come rust,
But still lies pointed as it plowed the dust.
If we who sight along it round the world,
See nothing worthy to have been its mark,
It is because like men we look too near,
Forgetting that as fitted to the sphere,
Our missiles always make too short an arc.
They fall, they rip the grass, they intersect
The curve of earth, and striking, break their own;
They make us cringe for metal-point on stone.
But this we know, the obstacle that checked
And tripped the body, shot the spirit on
Further than target ever showed or shone.

Asking For Roses

A house that lacks, seemingly, mistress and master,
  With doors that none but the wind ever closes,
  Its floor all littered with glass and with plaster;
  It stands in a garden of old-fashioned roses.

  I pass by that way in the gloaming with Mary;
  'I wonder,' I say, 'who the owner of those is.'
  'Oh, no one you know,' she answers me airy,
  'But one we must ask if we want any roses.'

So we must join hands in the dew coming coldly
  There in the hush of the wood that reposes,
  And turn and go up to the open door boldly,
  And knock to the echoes as beggars for roses.

'Pray, are you within there, Mistress Who-were-you? '
  'Tis Mary that speaks and our errand discloses.
  'Pray, are you within there? Bestir you, bestir you!
  'Tis summer again; there's two come for roses.

  'A word with you, that of the singer recalling-
  Old Herrick: a saying that every maid knows is
  A flower unplucked is but left to the falling,
  And nothing is gained by not gathering roses.'

  We do not loosen our hands' intertwining
  (Not caring so very much what she supposes) ,
  There when she comes on us mistily shining
  And grants us by silence the boon of her roses.

A Brook In The City

The farmhouse lingers, though averse to square
With the new city street it has to wear
A number in. But what about the brook
That held the house as in an elbow-crook?

I ask as one who knew the brook, its strength
And impulse, having dipped a finger length
And made it leap my knuckle, having tossed
A flower to try its currents where they crossed.
The meadow grass could be cemented down
From growing under pavements of a town;
The apple trees be sent to hearth-stone flame.
Is water wood to serve a brook the same?
How else dispose of an immortal force
No longer needed? Staunch it at its source
With cinder loads dumped down? The brook was thrown
Deep in a sewer dungeon under stone
In fetid darkness still to live and run --
And all for nothing it had ever done
Except forget to go in fear perhaps.
No one would know except for ancient maps
That such a brook ran water. But I wonder
If from its being kept forever under,
The thoughts may not have risen that so keep
This new-built city from both work and sleep.

A Patch Of Old Snow

There's a patch of old snow in a corner
That I should have guessed
Was a blow-away paper the rain
Had brought to rest.

It is speckled with grime as if
Small print overspread it,
The news of a day I've forgotten --
If I ever read it.

A Boundless Moment

He halted in the wind, and - what was that
Far in the maples, pale, but not a ghost?
He stood there bringing March against his thought,
And yet too ready to believe the most.

'Oh, that's the Paradise-in-bloom,' I said;
And truly it was fair enough for flowers
had we but in us to assume in march
Such white luxuriance of May for ours.

We stood a moment so in a strange world,
Myself as one his own pretense deceives;
And then I said the truth (and we moved on) .
A young beech clinging to its last year's leaves.

A Time To Talk

When a friend calls to me from the road
And slows his horse to a meaning walk,
I don't stand still and look around
On all the hills I haven't hoed,
And shout from where I am, What is it?
No, not as there is a time to talk.
I thrust my hoe in the mellow ground,
Blade-end up and five feet tall,
And plod: I go up to the stone wall
For a friendly visit.

Desert Places

Snow falling and night falling fast, oh, fast
In a field I looked into going past,
And the ground almost covered smooth in snow,
But a few weeds and stubble showing last.

The woods around it have it - it is theirs.
All animals are smothered in their lairs.
I am too absent-spirited to count;
The loneliness includes me unawares.

And lonely as it is, that loneliness
Will be more lonely ere it will be less -
A blanker whiteness of benighted snow
WIth no expression, nothing to express.

They cannot scare me with their empty spaces
Between stars - on stars where no human race is.
I have it in me so much nearer home
To scare myself with my own desert places.

After Apple Picking

My long two-pointed ladder's sticking through a tree
Toward heaven still.
And there's a barrel that I didn't fill
Beside it, and there may be two or three

Apples I didn't pick upon some bough.
But I am done with apple-picking now.
Essence of winter sleep is on the night,
The scent of apples; I am drowsing off.
I cannot shake the shimmer from my sight
I got from looking through a pane of glass
I skimmed this morning from the water-trough,
And held against the world of hoary grass.
It melted, and I let it fall and break.
But I was well
Upon my way to sleep before it fell,
And I could tell
What form my dreaming was about to take.
Magnified apples appear and reappear,
Stem end and blossom end,
And every fleck of russet showing clear.
My instep arch not only keeps the ache,
It keeps the pressure of a ladder-round.
And I keep hearing from the cellar-bin
That rumbling sound
Of load on load of apples coming in.
For I have had too much
Of apple-picking; I am overtired
Of the great harvest I myself desired.

There were ten thousand thousand fruit to touch,
Cherish in hand, lift down, and not let fall,
For all
That struck the earth,
No matter if not bruised, or spiked with stubble,
Went surely to the cider-apple heap
As of no worth.
One can see what will trouble
This sleep of mine, whatever sleep it is.
Were he not gone,
The woodchuck could say whether it's like his
Long sleep, as I describe its coming on,
Or just some human sleep.

Fireflies In The Garden

Here come real stars to fill the upper skies,
And here on earth come emulating flies,
That though they never equal stars in size,
(And they were never really stars at heart)
Achieve at times a very star-like start.
Only, of course, they can't sustain the part.

Birches

When I see birches bend to left and right
Across the lines of straighter darker trees,
I like to think some boy's been swinging them.
But swinging doesn't bend them down to stay.

Ice-storms do that. Often you must have seen them
Loaded with ice a sunny winter morning
After a rain. They click upon themselves
As the breeze rises, and turn many-coloured
As the stir cracks and crazes their enamel.
Soon the sun's warmth makes them shed crystal shells
Shattering and avalanching on the snow-crust
Such heaps of broken glass to sweep away
You'd think the inner dome of heaven had fallen.
They are dragged to the withered bracken by the load,
And they seem not to break; though once they are bowed
So low for long, they never right themselves:
You may see their trunks arching in the woods
Years afterwards, trailing their leaves on the ground,
Like girls on hands and knees that throw their hair
Before them over their heads to dry in the sun.
But I was going to say when Truth broke in
With all her matter-of-fact about the ice-storm,
I should prefer to have some boy bend them
As he went out and in to fetch the cows-
Some boy too far from town to learn baseball,
Whose only play was what he found himself,
Summer or winter, and could play alone.
One by one he subdued his father's trees

By riding them down over and over again
Until he took the stiffness out of them,
And not one but hung limp, not one was left
For him to conquer. He learned all there was
To learn about not launching out too soon
And so not carrying the tree away
Clear to the ground. He always kept his poise
To the top branches, climbing carefully
With the same pains you use to fill a cup
Up to the brim, and even above the brim.
Then he flung outward, feet first, with a swish,
Kicking his way down through the air to the ground.
So was I once myself a swinger of birches.
And so I dream of going back to be.
It's when I'm weary of considerations,
And life is too much like a pathless wood
Where your face burns and tickles with the cobwebs
Broken across it, and one eye is weeping
From a twig's having lashed across it open.
I'd like to get away from earth awhile
And then come back to it and begin over.
May no fate willfully misunderstand me
And half grant what I wish and snatch me away
Not to return. Earth's the right place for love:
I don't know where it's likely to go better.
I'd like to go by climbing a birch tree
And climb black branches up a snow-white trunk
Toward heaven, till the tree could bear no more,
But dipped its top and set me down again.
That would be good both going and coming back.
One could do worse than be a swinger of birches.

Mending Wall

Something there is that doesn't love a wall,
That sends the frozen-ground-swell under it,
And spills the upper boulders in the sun;
And makes gaps even two can pass abreast.

The work of hunters is another thing:
I have come after them and made repair
Where they have left not one stone on a stone,
But they would have the rabbit out of hiding,
To please the yelping dogs. The gaps I mean,
No one has seen them made or heard them made,
But at spring mending-time we find them there.
I let my neighbour know beyond the hill;
And on a day we meet to walk the line
And set the wall between us once again.
We keep the wall between us as we go.
To each the boulders that have fallen to each.
And some are loaves and some so nearly balls
We have to use a spell to make them balance:
"Stay where you are until our backs are turned!"
We wear our fingers rough with handling them.
Oh, just another kind of out-door game,
One on a side. It comes to little more:
There where it is we do not need the wall:
He is all pine and I am apple orchard.
My apple trees will never get across
And eat the cones under his pines, I tell him.
He only says, "Good fences make good neighbours."
Spring is the mischief in me, and I wonder

If I could put a notion in his head:
"Why do they make good neighbours? Isn't it
Where there are cows? But here there are no cows.
Before I built a wall I'd ask to know
What I was walling in or walling out,
And to whom I was like to give offence.
Something there is that doesn't love a wall,
That wants it down." I could say "Elves" to him,
But it's not elves exactly, and I'd rather
He said it for himself. I see him there
Bringing a stone grasped firmly by the top
In each hand, like an old-stone savage armed.
He moves in darkness as it seems to me,
Not of woods only and the shade of trees.
He will not go behind his father's saying,
And he likes having thought of it so well
He says again, "Good fences make good neighbours."

A Considerable Speck

A speck that would have been beneath my sight
On any but a paper sheet so white

Set off across what I had written there.
And I had idly poised my pen in air
To stop it with a period of ink
When something strange about it made me think,
This was no dust speck by my breathing blown,
But unmistakably a living mite
With inclinations it could call its own.
It paused as with suspicion of my pen,
And then came racing wildly on again
To where my manuscript was not yet dry;
Then paused again and either drank or smelt--
With loathing, for again it turned to fly.
Plainly with an intelligence I dealt.
It seemed too tiny to have room for feet,
Yet must have had a set of them complete
To express how much it didn't want to die.
It ran with terror and with cunning crept.
It faltered: I could see it hesitate;
Then in the middle of the open sheet
Cower down in desperation to accept
Whatever I accorded it of fate.
I have none of the tenderer-than-thou
Collectivistic regimenting love
With which the modern world is being swept.
But this poor microscopic item now!
Since it was nothing I knew evil of

I let it lie there till I hope it slept.

I have a mind myself and recognize
Mind when I meet with it in any guise
No one can know how glad I am to find
On any sheet the least display of mind.

In White: Frost's Early Version Of Design

A dented spider like a snow drop white
On a white Heal-all, holding up a moth
Like a white piece of lifeless satin cloth -
Saw ever curious eye so strange a sight? -
Portent in little, assorted death and blight
Like the ingredients of a witches' broth? -
The beady spider, the flower like a froth,
And the moth carried like a paper kite.

What had that flower to do with being white,
The blue prunella every child's delight.
What brought the kindred spider to that height?
(Make we no thesis of the miller's plight.)
What but design of darkness and of night?
Design, design! Do I use the word aright?

An Old Man's Winter Night

All out of doors looked darkly in at him
Through the thin frost, almost in separate stars,
That gathers on the pane in empty rooms.
What kept his eyes from giving back the gaze

Was the lamp tilted near them in his hand.
What kept him from remembering what it was
That brought him to that creaking room was age.
He stood with barrels round him -- at a loss.
And having scared the cellar under him
In clomping there, he scared it once again
In clomping off; -- and scared the outer night,
Which has its sounds, familiar, like the roar
Of trees and crack of branches, common things,
But nothing so like beating on a box.
A light he was to no one but himself
Where now he sat, concerned with he knew what,
A quiet light, and then not even that.
He consigned to the moon, such as she was,
So late-arising, to the broken moon
As better than the sun in any case
For such a charge, his snow upon the roof,
His icicles along the wall to keep;
And slept. The log that shifted with a jolt
Once in the stove, disturbed him and he shifted,
And eased his heavy breathing, but still slept.
One aged man -- one man -- can't keep a house,
A farm, a countryside, or if he can,
It's thus he does it of a winter night.

Bereft

Where had I heard this wind before
Change like this to a deeper roar?
What would it take my standing there for,
Holding open a restive door,
Looking down hill to a frothy shore?
Summer was past and the day was past.
Sombre clouds in the west were massed.
Out on the porch's sagging floor,
Leaves got up in a coil and hissed,
Blindly struck at my knee and missed.
Something sinister in the tone
Told me my secret must be known:
Word I was in the house alone
Somehow must have gotten abroad,
Word I was in my life alone,
Word I had no one left but God.

Devotion

The heart can think of no devotion
Greater than being shore to ocean -
Holding the curve of one position,
Counting an endless repetition.

Design

I found a dimpled spider, fat and white,
On a white heal-all, holding up a moth
Like a white piece of rigid satin cloth --
Assorted characters of death and blight
Mixed ready to begin the morning right,
Like the ingredients of a witches' broth --
A snow-drop spider, a flower like a froth,
And dead wings carried like a paper kite.

What had that flower to do with being white,
The wayside blue and innocent heal-all?
What brought the kindred spider to that height,
Then steered the white moth thither in the night?
What but design of darkness to appall?--
If design govern in a thing so small.

The Silken Tent

She is as in a field a silken tent
At midday when the sunny summer breeze
Has dried the dew and all its ropes relent,
So that in guys it gently sways at ease,
And its supporting central cedar pole,
That is its pinnacle to heavenward
And signifies the sureness of the soul,
Seems to owe naught to any single cord,
But strictly held by none, is loosely bound
By countless silken ties of love and thought
To every thing on earth the compass round,
And only by one's going slightly taut
In the capriciousness of summer air
Is of the slightlest bondage made aware.

A Line-Storm Song

The line-storm clouds fly tattered and swift,
The road is forlorn all day,
Where a myriad snowy quartz stones lift,
And the hoof-prints vanish away.
The roadside flowers, too wet for the bee,
Expend their bloom in vain.
Come over the hills and far with me,
And be my love in the rain.

The birds have less to say for themselves
In the wood-world's torn despair
Than now these numberless years the elves,
Although they are no less there:
All song of the woods is crushed like some
Wild, easily shattered rose.
Come, be my love in the wet woods; come,
Where the boughs rain when it blows.

There is the gale to urge behind
And bruit our singing down,
And the shallow waters aflutter with wind
From which to gather your gown.
What matter if we go clear to the west,
And come not through dry-shod?
For wilding brooch shall wet your breast
The rain-fresh goldenrod.

Oh, never this whelming east wind swells
But it seems like the sea's return

To the ancient lands where it left the shells
Before the age of the fern;
And it seems like the time when after doubt
Our love came back amain.
Oh, come forth into the storm and rout
And be my love in the rain.

Tree At My Window

Tree at my window, window tree,
My sash is lowered when night comes on;
But let there never be curtain drawn
Between you and me.

Vague dream head lifted out of the ground,
And thing next most diffuse to cloud,
Not all your light tongues talking aloud
Could be profound.

But tree, I have seen you taken and tossed,
And if you have seen me when I slept,
You have seen me when I was taken and swept
And all but lost.

That day she put our heads together,
Fate had her imagination about her,
Your head so much concerned with outer,
Mine with inner, weather.

A Cliff Dwelling

There sandy seems the golden sky
And golden seems the sandy plain.
No habitation meets the eye
Unless in the horizon rim,
Some halfway up the limestone wall,
That spot of black is not a stain
Or shadow, but a cavern hole,
Where someone used to climb and crawl
To rest from his besetting fears.
I see the callus on his soul
The disappearing last of him
And of his race starvation slim,
Oh years ago - ten thousand years.

Dust Of Snow

The way a crow
Shook down on me
The dust of snow
From a hemlock tree

Has given my heart
A change of mood
And saved some part
Of a day I had rued.

The Secret Sits

We dance round in a ring and suppose,
But the Secret sits in the middle and knows.

Come In

As I came to the edge of the woods,
Thrush music -- hark!
Now if it was dusk outside,
Inside it was dark.

Too dark in the woods for a bird
By sleight of wing
To better its perch for the night,
Though it still could sing.

The last of the light of the sun
That had died in the west
Still lived for one song more
In a thrush's breast.

Far in the pillared dark
Thrush music went --
Almost like a call to come in
To the dark and lament.

But no, I was out for stars;
I would not come in.
I meant not even if asked;
And I hadn't been.

A Servant to Servants

I didn't make you know how glad I was
To have you come and camp here on our land.
I promised myself to get down some day
And see the way you lived, but I don't know!

With a houseful of hungry men to feed
I guess you'd find.... It seems to me
I can't express my feelings any more
Than I can raise my voice or want to lift
My hand (oh, I can lift it when I have to).
Did ever you feel so? I hope you never.
It's got so I don't even know for sure
Whether I am glad, sorry, or anything.
There's nothing but a voice-like left inside
That seems to tell me how I ought to feel,
And would feel if I wasn't all gone wrong.
You take the lake. I look and look at it.
I see it's a fair, pretty sheet of water.
I stand and make myself repeat out loud
The advantages it has, so long and narrow,
Like a deep piece of some old running river
Cut short off at both ends. It lies five miles
Straight away through the mountain notch
From the sink window where I wash the plates,
And all our storms come up toward the house,
Drawing the slow waves whiter and whiter and whiter.
It took my mind off doughnuts and soda biscuit
To step outdoors and take the water dazzle
A sunny morning, or take the rising wind

About my face and body and through my wrapper,
When a storm threatened from the Dragon's Den,
And a cold chill shivered across the lake.
I see it's a fair, pretty sheet of water,
Our Willoughby! How did you hear of it?
I expect, though, everyone's heard of it.
In a book about ferns? Listen to that!
You let things more like feathers regulate
Your going and coming. And you like it here?
I can see how you might. But I don't know!
It would be different if more people came,
For then there would be business. As it is,
The cottages Len built, sometimes we rent them,
Sometimes we don't. We've a good piece of shore
That ought to be worth something, and may yet.
But I don't count on it as much as Len.
He looks on the bright side of everything,
Including me. He thinks I'll be all right
With doctoring. But it's not medicine--
Lowe is the only doctor's dared to say so--
It's rest I want--there, I have said it out--
From cooking meals for hungry hired men
And washing dishes after them--from doing
Things over and over that just won't stay done.
By good rights I ought not to have so much
Put on me, but there seems no other way.
Len says one steady pull more ought to do it.
He says the best way out is always through.
And I agree to that, or in so far
As that I can see no way out but through--
Leastways for me--and then they'll be convinced.
It's not that Len don't want the best for me.
It was his plan our moving over in
Beside the lake from where that day I showed you

We used to live--ten miles from anywhere.
We didn't change without some sacrifice,
But Len went at it to make up the loss.
His work's a man's, of course, from sun to sun,
But he works when he works as hard as I do--
Though there's small profit in comparisons.
(Women and men will make them all the same.)
But work ain't all. Len undertakes too much.
He's into everything in town. This year
It's highways, and he's got too many men
Around him to look after that make waste.
They take advantage of him shamefully,
And proud, too, of themselves for doing so.
We have four here to board, great good-for-nothings,
Sprawling about the kitchen with their talk
While I fry their bacon. Much they care!
No more put out in what they do or say
Than if I wasn't in the room at all.
Coming and going all the time, they are:
I don't learn what their names are, let alone
Their characters, or whether they are safe
To have inside the house with doors unlocked.
I'm not afraid of them, though, if they're not
Afraid of me. There's two can play at that.
I have my fancies: it runs in the family.
My father's brother wasn't right. They kept him
Locked up for years back there at the old farm.
I've been away once--yes, I've been away.
The State Asylum. I was prejudiced;
I wouldn't have sent anyone of mine there;
You know the old idea--the only asylum
Was the poorhouse, and those who could afford,
Rather than send their folks to such a place,
Kept them at home; and it does seem more human.

But it's not so: the place is the asylum.
There they have every means proper to do with,
And you aren't darkening other people's lives--
Worse than no good to them, and they no good
To you in your condition; you can't know
Affection or the want of it in that state.
I've heard too much of the old-fashioned way.
My father's brother, he went mad quite young.
Some thought he had been bitten by a dog,
Because his violence took on the form
Of carrying his pillow in his teeth;
But it's more likely he was crossed in love,
Or so the story goes. It was some girl.
Anyway all he talked about was love.
They soon saw he would do someone a mischief
If he wa'n't kept strict watch of, and it ended
In father's building him a sort of cage,
Or room within a room, of hickory poles,
Like stanchions in the barn, from floor to ceiling,--
A narrow passage all the way around.
Anything they put in for furniture
He'd tear to pieces, even a bed to lie on.
So they made the place comfortable with straw,
Like a beast's stall, to ease their consciences.
Of course they had to feed him without dishes.
They tried to keep him clothed, but he paraded
With his clothes on his arm--all of his clothes.
Cruel--it sounds. I 'spose they did the best
They knew. And just when he was at the height,
Father and mother married, and mother came,
A bride, to help take care of such a creature,
And accommodate her young life to his.
That was what marrying father meant to her.
She had to lie and hear love things made dreadful

By his shouts in the night. He'd shout and shout
Until the strength was shouted out of him,
And his voice died down slowly from exhaustion.
He'd pull his bars apart like bow and bow-string,
And let them go and make them twang until
His hands had worn them smooth as any ox-bow.
And then he'd crow as if he thought that child's play--
The only fun he had. I've heard them say, though,
They found a way to put a stop to it.
He was before my time--I never saw him;
But the pen stayed exactly as it was
There in the upper chamber in the ell,
A sort of catch-all full of attic clutter.
I often think of the smooth hickory bars.
It got so I would say--you know, half fooling--
"It's time I took my turn upstairs in jail"--
Just as you will till it becomes a habit.
No wonder I was glad to get away.
Mind you, I waited till Len said the word.
I didn't want the blame if things went wrong.
I was glad though, no end, when we moved out,
And I looked to be happy, and I was,
As I said, for a while--but I don't know!
Somehow the change wore out like a prescription.
And there's more to it than just window-views
And living by a lake. I'm past such help--
Unless Len took the notion, which he won't,
And I won't ask him--it's not sure enough.
I 'spose I've got to go the road I'm going:
Other folks have to, and why shouldn't I?
I almost think if I could do like you,
Drop everything and live out on the ground--
But it might be, come night, I shouldn't like it,
Or a long rain. I should soon get enough,

And be glad of a good roof overhead.
I've lain awake thinking of you, I'll warrant,
More than you have yourself, some of these nights.
The wonder was the tents weren't snatched away
From over you as you lay in your beds.
I haven't courage for a risk like that.
Bless you, of course, you're keeping me from work,
But the thing of it is, I need to be kept.
There's work enough to do--there's always that;
But behind's behind. The worst that you can do
Is set me back a little more behind.
I sha'n't catch up in this world, anyway.
I'd rather you'd not go unless you must.

God's Garden

God made a beatous garden
With lovely flowers strown,
But one straight, narrow pathway
That was not overgrown.

And to this beauteous garden
He brought mankind to live,
And said: 'To you, my children,
These lovely flowers I give.
Prune ye my vines and fig trees,
With care my flowerets tend,
But keep the pathway open
Your home is at the end.'

Then came another master,
Who did not love mankind,
And planted on the pathway
Gold flowers for them to find.
And mankind saw the bright flowers,
That, glitt'ring in the sun,
Quite hid the thorns of av'rice
That poison blood and bone;
And far off many wandered,
And when life's night came on,
They still were seeking gold flowers,
Lost, helpless and alone.

O, cease to heed the glamour
That blinds your foolish eyes,

Look upward to the glitter
Of stars in God's clear skies.
Their ways are pure and harmless
And will not lead astray,
Bid aid your erring footsteps
To keep the narrow way.
And when the sun shines brightly
Tend flowers that God has given
And keep the pathway open
That leads you on to heaven.

A Fountain, a Bottle, a Donkey's Ears, and Some Books

Old Davis owned a solid mica mountain
In Dalton that would someday make his fortune.
There'd been some Boston people out to see it:
And experts said that deep down in the mountain
The mica sheets were big as plate-glass windows.
He'd like to take me there and show it to me.

'I'll tell you what you show me. You remember
You said you knew the place where once, on Kinsman,
The early Mormons made a settlement
And built a stone baptismal font outdoors-
But Smith, or someone, called them off the mountain
To go West to a worse fight with the desert.
You said you'd seen the stone baptismal font.
Well, take me there.'

Someday I will.'

'Today.'

'Huh, that old bathtub, what is that to see?
Let's talk about it.'

'Let's go see the place.'

'To shut you up I'll tell you what I'll do:
I'll find that fountain if it takes all summer,

And both of our united strengths, to do it.'

'You've lost it, then?'

'Not so but I can find it.
No doubt it's grown up some to woods around it.
The mountain may have shifted since I saw it
In eighty-five.'

'As long ago as that?'

'If I remember rightly, it had sprung
A leak and emptied then. And forty years
Can do a good deal to bad masonry.
You won't see any Mormon swimming in it.
But you have said it, and we're off to find it.
Old as I am, I'm going to let myself
Be dragged by you all over everywhere- '
'I thought you were a guide.'

'I am a guide,
And that's why I can't decently refuse you.'

We made a day of it out of the world,
Ascending to descend to reascend.
The old man seriously took his bearings,
And spoke his doubts in every open place.

We came out on a look-off where we faced
A cliff, and on the cliff a bottle painted,
Or stained by vegetation from above,
A likeness to surprise the thrilly tourist.

'Well, if I haven't brought you to the fountain,
At least I've brought you to the famous Bottle.'

'I won't accept the substitute. It's empty.'

'So's everything.'

'I want my fountain.'

'I guess you'd find the fountain just as empty.
And anyway this tells me where I am.'

'Hadn't you long suspected where you were?'

'You mean miles from that Mormon settlement?
Look here, you treat your guide with due respect
If you don't want to spend the night outdoors.
I vow we must be near the place from where
The two converging slides, the avalanches,
On Marshall, look like donkey's ears.
We may as well see that and save the day.'

'Don't donkey's ears suggest we shake our own?'

'For God's sake, aren't you fond of viewing nature?
You don't like nature. All you like is books.
What signify a donkey's cars and bottle,
However natural? Give you your books!
Well then, right here is where I show you books.
Come straight down off this mountain just as fast
As we can fall and keep a-bouncing on our feet.
It's hell for knees unless done hell-for-leather.'

Be ready, I thought, for almost anything.

We struck a road I didn't recognize,
But welcomed for the chance to lave my shoes
In dust once more. We followed this a mile,

Perhaps, to where it ended at a house
I didn't know was there. It was the kind
To bring me to for broad-board paneling.
I never saw so good a house deserted.

'Excuse me if I ask you in a window
That happens to be broken, Davis said.
'The outside doors as yet have held against us.
I want to introduce you to the people
Who used to live here. They were Robinsons.
You must have heard of Clara Robinson,
The poetess who wrote the book of verses
And had it published. It was all about
The posies on her inner windowsill,
And the birds on her outer windowsill,
And how she tended both, or had them tended:
She never tended anything herself.
She was 'shut in' for life. She lived her whole
Life long in bed, and wrote her things in bed.
I'll show You how she had her sills extended
To entertain the birds and hold the flowers.
Our business first's up attic with her books.'

We trod uncomfortably on crunching glass
Through a house stripped of everything
Except, it seemed, the poetess's poems.
Books, I should say!- if books are what is needed.
A whole edition in a packing case
That, overflowing like a horn of plenty,
Or like the poetess's heart of love,
Had spilled them near the window, toward the light
Where driven rain had wet and swollen them.
Enough to stock a village library-
Unfortunately all of one kind, though.

They bad been brought home from some publisher
And taken thus into the family.
Boys and bad hunters had known what to do
With stone and lead to unprotected glass:
Shatter it inward on the unswept floors.
How had the tender verse escaped their outrage?
By being invisible for what it was,
Or else by some remoteness that defied them
To find out what to do to hurt a poem.
Yet oh! the tempting flatness of a book,
To send it sailing out the attic window
Till it caught wind and, opening out its covers,
Tried to improve on sailing like a tile
By flying like a bird (silent in flight,
But all the burden of its body song),
Only to tumble like a stricken bird,
And lie in stones and bushes unretrieved.
Books were not thrown irreverently about.
They simply lay where someone now and then,
Having tried one, had dropped it at his feet
And left it lying where it fell rejected.
Here were all those the poetess's life
Had been too short to sell or give away.

'Take one,' Old Davis bade me graciously.
'Why not take two or three?'
'Take all you want.'
Good-looking books like that.' He picked one fresh
In virgin wrapper from deep in the box,
And stroked it with a horny-handed kindness.
He read in one and I read in another,
Both either looking for or finding something.

The attic wasps went missing by like bullets.

I was soon satisfied for the time being.

All the way home I kept remembering
The small book in my pocket. It was there.
The poetess had sighed, I knew, in heaven
At having eased her heart of one more copy-
Legitimately. My demand upon her,
Though slight, was a demand. She felt the tug.
In time she would be rid of all her books.

Ghost House

I dwell in a lonely house I know
That vanished many a summer ago,
And left no trace but the cellar walls,
And a cellar in which the daylight falls,
And the purple-stemmed wild raspberries grow.

O'er ruined fences the grape-vines shield
The woods come back to the mowing field;
The orchard tree has grown one copse
Of new wood and old where the woodpecker chops;
The footpath down to the well is healed.

I dwell with a strangely aching heart
In that vanished abode there far apart
On that disused and forgotten road
That has no dust-bath now for the toad.
Night comes; the black bats tumble and dart;

The whippoorwill is coming to shout
And hush and cluck and flutter about:
I hear him begin far enough away
Full many a time to say his say
Before he arrives to say it out.

It is under the small, dim, summer star.
I know not who these mute folk are
Who share the unlit place with me--
Those stones out under the low-limbed tree
Doubtless bear names that the mosses mar.

They are tireless folk, but slow and sad,
Though two, close-keeping, are lass and lad,--
With none among them that ever sings,
And yet, in view of how many things,
As sweet companions as might be had.

54

Pan With Us

PAN came out of the woods one day,—
His skin and his hair and his eyes were gray,
The gray of the moss of walls were they,—
   And stood in the sun and looked his fill
   At wooded valley and wooded hill.

   He stood in the zephyr, pipes in hand,
   On a height of naked pasture land;
   In all the country he did command
He saw no smoke and he saw no roof.
That was well! and he stamped a hoof.

His heart knew peace, for none came here
   To this lean feeding save once a year
   Someone to salt the half-wild steer,
Or homespun children with clicking pails
   Who see no little they tell no tales.

   He tossed his pipes, too hard to teach
   A new-world song, far out of reach,
For a sylvan sign that the blue jay's screech
And the whimper of hawks beside the sun
   Were music enough for him, for one.

Times were changed from what they were:
   Such pipes kept less of power to stir
   The fruited bough of the juniper
   And the fragile bluets clustered there
Than the merest aimless breath of air.

They were pipes of pagan mirth,
And the world had found new terms of worth.
He laid him down on the sun-burned earth
And ravelled a flower and looked away—
Play? Play? —What should he play?

Good Hours

I had for my winter evening walk-
No one at all with whom to talk,
But I had the cottages in a row
Up to their shining eyes in snow.

And I thought I had the folk within:
I had the sound of a violin;
I had a glimpse through curtain laces
Of youthful forms and youthful faces.

I had such company outward bound.
I went till there were no cottages found.
I turned and repented, but coming back
I saw no window but that was black.

Over the snow my creaking feet
Disturbed the slumbering village street
Like profanation, by your leave,
At ten o'clock of a winter eve.

But Outer Space

But outer Space,
At least this far,
For all the fuss
Of the populace
Stays more popular
Than populous

Spring Pools

These pools that, though in forests, still reflect
The total sky almost without defect,
And like the flowers beside them, chill and shiver,
Will like the flowers beside them soon be gone,
And yet not out by any brook or river,
But up by roots to bring dark foliage on.

The trees that have it in their pent-up buds
To darken nature and be summer woods -
Let them think twice before they use their powers
To blot out and drink up and sweep away
These flowery waters and these watery flowers
From snow that melted only yesterday.

Evening In A Sugar Orchard

From where I lingered in a lull in March
outside the sugar-house one night for choice,
I called the fireman with a careful voice
And bade him leave the pan and stoke the arch:
'O fireman, give the fire another stoke,
And send more sparks up chimney with the smoke.'
I thought a few might tangle, as they did,
Among bare maple boughs, and in the rare
Hill atmosphere not cease to glow,
And so be added to the moon up there.
The moon, though slight, was moon enough to show
On every tree a bucket with a lid,
And on black ground a bear-skin rug of snow.
The sparks made no attempt to be the moon.
They were content to figure in the trees
As Leo, Orion, and the Pleiades.
And that was what the boughs were full of soon.

Stars

How countlessly they congregate
O'er our tumultuous snow,
Which flows in shapes as tall as trees
When wintry winds do blow!--

As if with keenness for our fate,
Our faltering few steps on
To white rest, and a place of rest
Invisible at dawn,--

And yet with neither love nor hate,
Those stars like some snow-white
Minerva's snow-white marble eyes
Without the gift of sight.

Once By The Pacific

The shattered water made a misty din.
Great waves looked over others coming in,
And thought of doing something to the shore
That water never did to land before.
The clouds were low and hairy in the skies,
Like locks blown forward in the gleam of eyes.
You could not tell, and yet it looked as if
The shore was lucky in being backed by cliff,
The cliff in being backed by continent;
It looked as if a night of dark intent
Was coming, and not only a night, an age.
Someone had better be prepared for rage.
There would be more than ocean-water broken
Before God's last Put out the light was spoken.

Home Burial

He saw her from the bottom of the stairs
Before she saw him. She was starting down,
Looking back over her shoulder at some fear.
She took a doubtful step and then undid it

To raise herself and look again. He spoke
Advancing toward her: "What is it you see
From up there always? -- for I want to know."
She turned and sank upon her skirts at that,
And her face changed from terrified to dull.
He said to gain time: "What is it you see?"
Mounting until she cowered under him.
"I will find out now -- you must tell me, dear."
She, in her place, refused him any help,
With the least stiffening of her neck and silence.
She let him look, sure that he wouldn't see,
Blind creature; and a while he didn't see.
But at last he murmured, "Oh" and again, "Oh."

"What is it -- what?" she said.

"Just that I see."

"You don't," she challenged. "Tell me what it is."

"The wonder is I didn't see at once.
I never noticed it from here before.
I must be wonted to it -- that's the reason.
The little graveyard where my people are!

So small the window frames the whole of it.
Not so much larger than a bedroom, is it?
There are three stones of slate and one of marble,
Broad-shouldered little slabs there in the sunlight
On the sidehill. We haven't to mind those.
But I understand: it is not the stones,
But the child's mound ----"

"Don't, don't, don't,
don't," she cried.

She withdrew, shrinking from beneath his arm
That rested on the banister, and slid downstairs;
And turned on him with such a daunting look,
He said twice over before he knew himself:
"Can't a man speak of his own child he's lost?"

"Not you! -- Oh, where's my hat? Oh, I don't need it!
I must get out of here. I must get air.--
I don't know rightly whether any man can."

"Amy! Don't go to someone else this time.
Listen to me. I won't come down the stairs."
He sat and fixed his chin between his fists.
"There's something I should like to ask you, dear."

"You don't know how to ask it."
"Help me, then."

Her fingers moved the latch for all reply.

"My words are nearly always an offense.
I don't know how to speak of anything
So as to please you. But I might be taught,

I should suppose. I can't say I see how.
A man must partly give up being a man
With womenfolk. We could have some arrangement
By which I'd bind myself to keep hands off
Anything special you're a-mind to name.
Though I don't like such things 'twixt those that love.
Two that don't love can't live together without them.
But two that do can't live together with them."
She moved the latch a little. "Don't -- don't go.
Don't carry it to someone else this time.
Tell me about it if it's something human.
Let me into your grief. I'm not so much
Unlike other folks as your standing there
Apart would make me out. Give me my chance.
I do think, though, you overdo it a little.
What was it brought you up to think it the thing
To take your mother-loss of a first child
So inconsolably -- in the face of love.
You'd think his memory might be satisfied ----"

"There you go sneering now!"

"I'm not, I'm not!
You make me angry. I'll come down to you.
God, what a woman! And it's come to this,
A man can't speak of his own child that's dead."

"You can't because you don't know how to speak.
If you had any feelings, you that dug
With your own hand -- how could you? -- his little grave;
I saw you from that very window there,
Making the gravel leap and leap in air,
Leap up, like that, like that, and land so lightly
And roll back down the mound beside the hole.

I thought, Who is that man? I didn't know you.
And I crept down the stairs and up the stairs
To look again, and still your spade kept lifting.
Then you came in. I heard your rumbling voice
Out in the kitchen, and I don't know why,
But I went near to see with my own eyes.
You could sit there with the stains on your shoes
Of the fresh earth from your own baby's grave
And talk about your everyday concerns.
You had stood the spade up against the wall
Outside there in the entry, for I saw it."

"I shall laugh the worst laugh I ever laughed.
I'm cursed. God, if I don't believe I'm cursed."

"I can repeat the very words you were saying:
'Three foggy mornings and one rainy day
Will rot the best birch fence a man can build.'
Think of it, talk like that at such a time!
What had how long it takes a birch to rot
To do with what was in the darkened parlour?
You couldn't care! The nearest friends can go
With anyone to death, comes so far short
They might as well not try to go at all.
No, from the time when one is sick to death,
One is alone, and he dies more alone.
Friends make pretense of following to the grave,
But before one is in it, their minds are turned
And making the best of their way back to life
And living people, and things they understand.
But the world's evil. I won't have grief so
If I can change it. Oh, I won't, I won't!"

"There, you have said it all and you feel better.

You won't go now. You're crying. Close the door.
The heart's gone out of it: why keep it up?
Amy! There's someone coming down the road!"

"You -- oh, you think the talk is all. I must go --
Somewhere out of this house. How can I make you ----"

"If -- you -- do!" She was opening the door wider.
"Where do you mean to go? First tell me that.
I'll follow and bring you back by force. I will! --"

Two Tramps In Mud Time

Out of the mud two strangers came
And caught me splitting wood in the yard,
And one of them put me off my aim
By hailing cheerily "Hit them hard!"
I knew pretty well why he had dropped behind
And let the other go on a way.
I knew pretty well what he had in mind:
He wanted to take my job for pay.

Good blocks of oak it was I split,
As large around as the chopping block;
And every piece I squarely hit
Fell splinterless as a cloven rock.
The blows that a life of self-control
Spares to strike for the common good,
That day, giving a loose my soul,
I spent on the unimportant wood.

The sun was warm but the wind was chill.
You know how it is with an April day
When the sun is out and the wind is still,
You're one month on in the middle of May.
But if you so much as dare to speak,
A cloud comes over the sunlit arch,
A wind comes off a frozen peak,
And you're two months back in the middle of March.

A bluebird comes tenderly up to alight

And turns to the wind to unruffle a plume,
His song so pitched as not to excite
A single flower as yet to bloom.
It is snowing a flake; and he half knew
Winter was only playing possum.
Except in color he isn't blue,
But he wouldn't advise a thing to blossom.

The water for which we may have to look
In summertime with a witching wand,
In every wheelrut's now a brook,
In every print of a hoof a pond.
Be glad of water, but don't forget
The lurking frost in the earth beneath
That will steal forth after the sun is set
And show on the water its crystal teeth.

The time when most I loved my task
The two must make me love it more
By coming with what they came to ask.
You'd think I never had felt before
The weight of an ax-head poised aloft,
The grip of earth on outspread feet,
The life of muscles rocking soft
And smooth and moist in vernal heat.

Out of the wood two hulking tramps
(From sleeping God knows where last night,
But not long since in the lumber camps).
They thought all chopping was theirs of right.
Men of the woods and lumberjacks,
They judged me by their appropriate tool.
Except as a fellow handled an ax
They had no way of knowing a fool.

Nothing on either side was said.
They knew they had but to stay their stay

And all their logic would fill my head:
As that I had no right to play
With what was another man's work for gain.
My right might be love but theirs was need.
And where the two exist in twain
Theirs was the better right--agreed.

But yield who will to their separation,
My object in living is to unite
My avocation and my vocation
As my two eyes make one in sight.
Only where love and need are one,
And the work is play for mortal stakes,
Is the deed ever really done
For Heaven and the future's sakes.

October

O hushed October morning mild,
Thy leaves have ripened to the fall;
Tomorrow's wind, if it be wild,
Should waste them all.

The crows above the forest call;
Tomorrow they may form and go.
O hushed October morning mild,
Begin the hours of this day slow.
Make the day seem to us less brief.
Hearts not averse to being beguiled,
Beguile us in the way you know.
Release one leaf at break of day;
At noon release another leaf;
One from our trees, one far away.
Retard the sun with gentle mist;
Enchant the land with amethyst.
Slow, slow!
For the grapes' sake, if the were all,
Whose elaves already are burnt with frost,
Whose clustered fruit must else be lost—
For the grapes' sake along the all.

Carpe Diem

Age saw two quiet children
Go loving by at twilight,
He knew not whether homeward,
Or outward from the village,

Or (chimes were ringing) churchward,
He waited, (they were strangers)
Till they were out of hearing
To bid them both be happy.
'Be happy, happy, happy,
And seize the day of pleasure.'
The age-long theme is Age's.
'Twas Age imposed on poems
Their gather-roses burden
To warn against the danger
That overtaken lovers
From being overflooded
With happiness should have it.
And yet not know they have it.
But bid life seize the present?
It lives less in the present
Than in the future always,
And less in both together
Than in the past. The present
Is too much for the senses,
Too crowding, too confusing-
Too present to imagine.

Flower-Gathering

I left you in the morning,
And in the morning glow,
You walked a way beside me
To make me sad to go.
Do you know me in the gloaming,
Gaunt and dusty gray with roaming?
Are you dumb because you know me not,
Or dumb because you know?

All for me And not a question
For the faded flowers gay
That could take me from beside you
For the ages of a day?
They are yours, and be the measure
Of their worth for you to treasure,
The measure of the little while
That I've been long away.

Bond And Free

Love has earth to which she clings
With hills and circling arms about-
Wall within wall to shut fear out.
But Thought has need of no such things,
For Thought has a pair of dauntless wings.

On snow and sand and turn, I see
Where Love has left a printed trace
With straining in the world's embrace.
And such is Love and glad to be
But Thought has shaken his ankles free.

Thought cleaves the interstellar gloom
And sits in Sirius' disc all night,
Till day makes him retrace his flight
With smell of burning on every plume,
Back past the sun to an earthly room.

His gains in heaven are what they are.
Yet some say Love by being thrall
And simply staying possesses all
In several beauty that Thought fares far
To find fused in another star.

Good-Bye, And Keep Cold

This saying good-bye on the edge of the dark
And cold to an orchard so young in the bark
Reminds me of all that can happen to harm
An orchard away at the end of the farm
All winter, cut off by a hill from the house.
I don't want it girdled by rabbit and mouse,
I don't want it dreamily nibbled for browse
By deer, and I don't want it budded by grouse.
(If certain it wouldn't be idle to call
I'd summon grouse, rabbit, and deer to the wall
And warn them away with a stick for a gun.)
I don't want it stirred by the heat of the sun.
(We made it secure against being, I hope,
By setting it out on a northerly slope.)
No orchard's the worse for the wintriest storm;
But one thing about it, it mustn't get warm.
"How often already you've had to be told,
Keep cold, young orchard. Good-bye and keep cold.
Dread fifty above more than fifty below."
I have to be gone for a season or so.
My business awhile is with different trees,
Less carefully nourished, less fruitful than these,
And such as is done to their wood with an axe--
Maples and birches and tamaracks.
I wish I could promise to lie in the night
And think of an orchard's arboreal plight
When slowly (and nobody comes with a light)
Its heart sinks lower under the sod.
But something has to be left to God.

The Gift Outright

The land was ours before we were the land's.
She was our land more than a hundred years
Before we were her people. She was ours
In Massachusetts, in Virginia,
But we were England's, still colonials,
Possessing what we still were unpossessed by,
Possessed by what we now no more possessed.
Something we were withholding made us weak
Until we found out that it was ourselves
We were withholding from our land of living,
And forthwith found salvation in surrender.
Such as we were we gave ourselves outright
(The deed of gift was many deeds of war)
To the land vaguely realizing westward,
But still unstoried, artless, unenhanced,
Such as she was, such as she would become.

Revelation

We make ourselves a place apart
Behind light words that tease and flout,
But oh, the agitated heart
Till someone find us really out.

'Tis pity if the case require
(Or so we say) that in the end
We speak the literal to inspire
The understanding of a friend.

But so with all, from babes that play
At hide-and-seek to God afar,
So all who hide too well away
Must speak and tell us where they are.

The Sound Of Trees

I wonder about the trees.
Why do we wish to bear
Forever the noise of these
More than another noise

So close to our dwelling place?
We suffer them by the day
Till we lose all measure of pace,
And fixity in our joys,
And acquire a listening air.
They are that that talks of going
But never gets away;
And that talks no less for knowing,
As it grows wiser and older,
That now it means to stay.
My feet tug at the floor
And my head sways to my shoulder
Sometimes when I watch trees sway,
From the window or the door.
I shall set forth for somewhere,
I shall make the reckless choice
Some day when they are in voice
And tossing so as to scare
The white clouds over them on.
I shall have less to say,
But I shall be gone.

My Butterfly

Thine emulous fond flowers are dead, too,
And the daft sun-assaulter, he
That frighted thee so oft, is fled or dead:
Save only me

(Nor is it sad to thee!)
Save only me
There is none left to mourn thee in the fields.
The gray grass is not dappled with the snow;
Its two banks have not shut upon the river;
But it is long ago-
It seems forever-
Since first I saw thee glance,
With all the dazzling other ones,
In airy dalliance,
Precipitate in love,
Tossed, tangled, whirled and whirled above,
Like a limp rose-wreath in a fairy dance.
When that was, the soft mist
Of my regret hung not on all the land,
And I was glad for thee,
And glad for me, I wist.
Thou didst not know, who tottered, wandering on high,
That fate had made thee for the pleasure of the wind,
With those great careless wings,
Nor yet did I.
And there were other things:
It seemed God let thee flutter from his gentle clasp:
Then fearful he had let thee win

Too far beyond him to be gathered in,
Snatched thee, o'er eager, with ungentle grasp.
Ah! I remember me
How once conspiracy was rife
Against my life-
The languor of it and the dreaming fond;
Surging, the grasses dizzied me of thought,
The breeze three odors brought,
And a gem-flower waved in a wand!
Then when I was distraught
And could not speak,
Sidelong, full on my cheek,
What should that reckless zephyr fling
But the wild touch of thy dye-dusty wing!
I found that wing broken to-day!
For thou are dead, I said,
And the strange birds say.
I found it with the withered leaves
Under the eaves.

God's Garden

God made a beatous garden
With lovely flowers strown,
But one straight, narrow pathway
That was not overgrown.

And to this beauteous garden
He brought mankind to live,
And said: 'To you, my children,
These lovely flowers I give.
Prune ye my vines and fig trees,
With care my flowerets tend,
But keep the pathway open
Your home is at the end.'

Then came another master,
Who did not love mankind,
And planted on the pathway
Gold flowers for them to find.
And mankind saw the bright flowers,
That, glitt'ring in the sun,
Quite hid the thorns of av'rice
That poison blood and bone;
And far off many wandered,
And when life's night came on,
They still were seeking gold flowers,
Lost, helpless and alone.

O, cease to heed the glamour
That blinds your foolish eyes,

Look upward to the glitter
Of stars in God's clear skies.
Their ways are pure and harmless
And will not lead astray,
Bid aid your erring footsteps
To keep the narrow way.
And when the sun shines brightly
Tend flowers that God has given
And keep the pathway open
That leads you on to heaven.

The Aim Was Song

Before man to blow to right
The wind once blew itself untaught,
And did its loudest day and night
In any rough place where it caught.

Man came to tell it what was wrong:
It hadn't found the place to blow;
It blew too hard - the aim was song.
And listen - how it ought to go!

He took a little in his mouth,
And held it long enough for north
To be converted into south,
And then by measure blew it forth.

By measure. It was word and note,
The wind the wind had meant to be -
A little through the lips and throat.
The aim was song - the wind could see.

Now Close The Windows

Now close the windows and hush all the fields:
If the trees must, let them silently toss;
No bird is singing now, and if there is,
Be it my loss.

It will be long ere the marshes resume,
I will be long ere the earliest bird:
So close the windows and not hear the wind,
But see all wind-stirred.

Two Look At Two

Love and forgetting might have carried them
A little further up the mountain side
With night so near, but not much further up.
They must have halted soon in any case

With thoughts of a path back, how rough it was
With rock and washout, and unsafe in darkness;
When they were halted by a tumbled wall
With barbed-wire binding. They stood facing this,
Spending what onward impulse they still had
In One last look the way they must not go,
On up the failing path, where, if a stone
Or earthslide moved at night, it moved itself;
No footstep moved it. 'This is all,' they sighed,
Good-night to woods.' But not so; there was more.
A doe from round a spruce stood looking at them
Across the wall, as near the wall as they.
She saw them in their field, they her in hers.
The difficulty of seeing what stood still,
Like some up-ended boulder split in two,
Was in her clouded eyes; they saw no fear there.
She seemed to think that two thus they were safe.
Then, as if they were something that, though strange,
She could not trouble her mind with too long,
She sighed and passed unscared along the wall.
'This, then, is all. What more is there to ask?'
But no, not yet. A snort to bid them wait.
A buck from round the spruce stood looking at them
Across the wall as near the wall as they.

This was an antlered buck of lusty nostril,
Not the same doe come back into her place.
He viewed them quizzically with jerks of head,
As if to ask, 'Why don't you make some motion?
Or give some sign of life? Because you can't.
I doubt if you're as living as you look."
Thus till he had them almost feeling dared
To stretch a proffering hand -- and a spell-breaking.
Then he too passed unscared along the wall.
Two had seen two, whichever side you spoke from.
'This must be all.' It was all. Still they stood,
A great wave from it going over them,
As if the earth in one unlooked-for favour
Had made them certain earth returned their love.

The Tuft Of Flowers

I went to turn the grass once after one
Who mowed it in the dew before the sun.

The dew was gone that made his blade so keen

Before I came to view the levelled scene.

I looked for him behind an isle of trees;
I listened for his whetstone on the breeze.

But he had gone his way, the grass all mown,
And I must be, as he had been,—alone,

'As all must be,' I said within my heart,
'Whether they work together or apart.'

But as I said it, swift there passed me by
On noiseless wing a bewildered butterfly,

Seeking with memories grown dim over night
Some resting flower of yesterday's delight.

And once I marked his flight go round and round,
As where some flower lay withering on the ground.

And then he flew as far as eye could see,
And then on tremulous wing came back to me.

I thought of questions that have no reply,

And would have turned to toss the grass to dry;

But he turned first, and led my eye to look
At a tall tuft of flowers beside a brook,

A leaping tongue of bloom the scythe had spared
Beside a reedy brook the scythe had bared.

I left my place to know them by their name,
Finding them butterfly-weed when I came.

The mower in the dew had loved them thus,
By leaving them to flourish, not for us,

Nor yet to draw one thought of ours to him,
But from sheer morning gladness at the brim.

The butterfly and I had lit upon,
Nevertheless, a message from the dawn,

That made me hear the wakening birds around,
And hear his long scythe whispering to the ground,

And feel a spirit kindred to my own;
So that henceforth I worked no more alone;

But glad with him, I worked as with his aid,
And weary, sought at noon with him the shade;

And dreaming, as it were, held brotherly speech
With one whose thought I had not hoped to reach.

'Men work together,' I told him from the heart,
'Whether they work together or apart.'

Neither Out Far Nor In Deep

The people along the sand
All turn and look one way.
They turn their back on the land.
They look at the sea all day.

As long as it takes to pass
A ship keeps raising its hull;
The wetter ground like glass
Reflects a standing gull

The land may vary more;
But wherever the truth may be-
The water comes ashore,
And the people look at the sea.

They cannot look out far.
They cannot look in deep.
But when was that ever a bar
To any watch they keep?

Never Again Would Bird's Song Be The Same

He would declare and could himself believe
That the birds there in all the garden round
From having heard the daylong voice of Eve
Had added to their own an oversound,
Her tone of meaning but without the words.
Admittedly an eloquence so soft
Could only have had an influence on birds
When call or laughter carried it aloft.
Be that as may be, she was in their song.
Moreover her voice upon their voices crossed
Had now persisted in the woods so long
That probably it never would be lost.
Never again would birds' song be the same.
And to do that to birds was why she came.

Mowing

There was never a sound beside the wood but one,
And that was my long scythe whispering to the ground.
What was it it whispered? I knew not well myself;
Perhaps it was something about the heat of the sun,
Something, perhaps, about the lack of sound--
And that was why it whispered and did not speak.
It was no dream of the gift of idle hours,
Or easy gold at the hand of fay or elf:
Anything more than the truth would have seemed too weak
To the earnest love that laid the swale in rows,
Not without feeble-pointed spikes of flowers
(Pale orchises), and scared a bright green snake.
The fact is the sweetest dream that labour knows.
My long scythe whispered and left the hay to make.

Fragmentary Blue

Why make so much of fragmentary blue
In here and there a bird, or butterfly,
Or flower, or wearing-stone, or open eye,
When heaven presents in sheets the solid hue?

Since earth is earth, perhaps, not heaven (as yet)--
Though some savants make earth include the sky;
And blue so far above us comes so high,
It only gives our wish for blue a whet.

Into My Own

One of my wishes is that those dark trees,
So old and firm they scarcely show the breeze,
Were not, as 'twere, the merest mask of gloom,
But stretched away unto the edge of doom.

I should not be withheld but that some day
into their vastness I should steal away,
Fearless of ever finding open land,
or highway where the slow wheel pours the sand.

I do not see why I should e'er turn back,
Or those should not set forth upon my track
To overtake me, who should miss me here
And long to know if still I held them dear.

They would not find me changed from him they knew--
Only more sure of all I though was true.

On Looking Up By Chance At The Constellations

You'll wait a long, long time for anything much
To happen in heaven beyond the floats of cloud
And the Northern Lights that run like tingling nerves.
The sun and moon get crossed, but they never touch,
Nor strike out fire from each other nor crash out loud.
The planets seem to interfere in their curves -
But nothing ever happens, no harm is done.
We may as well go patiently on with our life,
And look elsewhere than to stars and moon and sun
For the shocks and changes we need to keep us sane.
It is true the longest drout will end in rain,
The longest peace in China will end in strife.
Still it wouldn't reward the watcher to stay awake
In hopes of seeing the calm of heaven break
On his particular time and personal sight.
That calm seems certainly safe to last to-night.

The Death Of The Hired Man

Mary sat musing on the lamp-flame at the table
Waiting for Warren. When she heard his step,
She ran on tip-toe down the darkened passage
To meet him in the doorway with the news
And put him on his guard. "Silas is back."
She pushed him outward with her through the door
And shut it after her. "Be kind," she said.
She took the market things from Warren's arms
And set them on the porch, then drew him down
To sit beside her on the wooden steps.

"When was I ever anything but kind to him?
But I'll not have the fellow back," he said.
"I told him so last haying, didn't I?
'If he left then,' I said, 'that ended it.'
What good is he? Who else will harbour him
At his age for the little he can do?
What help he is there's no depending on.
Off he goes always when I need him most.
'He thinks he ought to earn a little pay,
Enough at least to buy tobacco with,
So he won't have to beg and be beholden.'
'All right,' I say, 'I can't afford to pay
Any fixed wages, though I wish I could.'
'Someone else can.' 'Then someone else will have to.'
I shouldn't mind his bettering himself
If that was what it was. You can be certain,
When he begins like that, there's someone at him
Trying to coax him off with pocket-money,--

In haying time, when any help is scarce.
In winter he comes back to us. I'm done."

"Sh! not so loud: he'll hear you," Mary said.

"I want him to: he'll have to soon or late."

"He's worn out. He's asleep beside the stove.
When I came up from Rowe's I found him here,
Huddled against the barn-door fast asleep,
A miserable sight, and frightening, too--
You needn't smile--I didn't recognise him--
I wasn't looking for him--and he's changed.
Wait till you see."

"Where did you say he'd been?"

"He didn't say. I dragged him to the house,
And gave him tea and tried to make him smoke.
I tried to make him talk about his travels.
Nothing would do: he just kept nodding off."

"What did he say? Did he say anything?"

"But little."

"Anything? Mary, confess
He said he'd come to ditch the meadow for me."

"Warren!"
"But did he? I just want to know."

"Of course he did. What would you have him say?
Surely you wouldn't grudge the poor old man

Some humble way to save his self-respect.
He added, if you really care to know,
He meant to clear the upper pasture, too.
That sounds like something you have heard before?
Warren, I wish you could have heard the way
He jumbled everything. I stopped to look
Two or three times--he made me feel so queer--
To see if he was talking in his sleep.
He ran on Harold Wilson--you remember--
The boy you had in haying four years since.
He's finished school, and teaching in his college.
Silas declares you'll have to get him back.
He says they two will make a team for work:
Between them they will lay this farm as smooth!
The way he mixed that in with other things.
He thinks young Wilson a likely lad, though daft
On education--you know how they fought
All through July under the blazing sun,
Silas up on the cart to build the load,
Harold along beside to pitch it on."

"Yes, I took care to keep well out of earshot."

"Well, those days trouble Silas like a dream.
You wouldn't think they would. How some things linger!
Harold's young college boy's assurance piqued him.
After so many years he still keeps finding
Good arguments he sees he might have used.
I sympathise. I know just how it feels
To think of the right thing to say too late.
Harold's associated in his mind with Latin.
He asked me what I thought of Harold's saying
He studied Latin like the violin
Because he liked it--that an argument!

He said he couldn't make the boy believe
He could find water with a hazel prong--
Which showed how much good school had ever done him.
He wanted to go over that. But most of all
He thinks if he could have another chance
To teach him how to build a load of hay----"

"I know, that's Silas' one accomplishment.
He bundles every forkful in its place,
And tags and numbers it for future reference,
So he can find and easily dislodge it
In the unloading. Silas does that well.
He takes it out in bunches like big birds' nests.
You never see him standing on the hay
He's trying to lift, straining to lift himself."

"He thinks if he could teach him that, he'd be
Some good perhaps to someone in the world.
He hates to see a boy the fool of books.
Poor Silas, so concerned for other folk,
And nothing to look backward to with pride,
And nothing to look forward to with hope,
So now and never any different."

Part of a moon was falling down the west,
Dragging the whole sky with it to the hills.
Its light poured softly in her lap. She saw
And spread her apron to it. She put out her hand
Among the harp-like morning-glory strings,
Taut with the dew from garden bed to eaves,
As if she played unheard the tenderness
That wrought on him beside her in the night.
"Warren," she said, "he has come home to die:
You needn't be afraid he'll leave you this time."

"Home," he mocked gently.

"Yes, what else but home?
It all depends on what you mean by home.
Of course he's nothing to us, any more
Than was the hound that came a stranger to us
Out of the woods, worn out upon the trail."

"Home is the place where, when you have to go there,
They have to take you in."

"I should have called it
Something you somehow haven't to deserve."

Warren leaned out and took a step or two,
Picked up a little stick, and brought it back
And broke it in his hand and tossed it by.
"Silas has better claim on us you think
Than on his brother? Thirteen little miles
As the road winds would bring him to his door.
Silas has walked that far no doubt to-day.
Why didn't he go there? His brother's rich,
A somebody--director in the bank."

"He never told us that."

"We know it though."

"I think his brother ought to help, of course.
I'll see to that if there is need. He ought of right
To take him in, and might be willing to--
He may be better than appearances.
But have some pity on Silas. Do you think

If he'd had any pride in claiming kin
Or anything he looked for from his brother,
He'd keep so still about him all this time?"

"I wonder what's between them."

"I can tell you.
Silas is what he is--we wouldn't mind him--
But just the kind that kinsfolk can't abide.
He never did a thing so very bad.
He don't know why he isn't quite as good
As anyone. He won't be made ashamed
To please his brother, worthless though he is."

"I can't think Si ever hurt anyone."

"No, but he hurt my heart the way he lay
And rolled his old head on that sharp-edged chair-back.
He wouldn't let me put him on the lounge.
You must go in and see what you can do.
I made the bed up for him there to-night.
You'll be surprised at him--how much he's broken.
His working days are done; I'm sure of it."

"I'd not be in a hurry to say that."

"I haven't been. Go, look, see for yourself.
But, Warren, please remember how it is:
He's come to help you ditch the meadow.
He has a plan. You mustn't laugh at him.
He may not speak of it, and then he may.
I'll sit and see if that small sailing cloud
Will hit or miss the moon."

It hit the moon.

Then there were three there, making a dim row,
The moon, the little silver cloud, and she.

Warren returned--too soon, it seemed to her,
Slipped to her side, caught up her hand and waited.

"Warren," she questioned.

"Dead," was all he answered.

The Wood-Pile

Out walking in the frozen swamp one gray day,
I paused and said, "I will turn back from here.
No, I will go on farther -- and we shall see."
The hard snow held me, save where now and then

One foot went through. The view was all in lines
Straight up and down of tall slim trees
Too much alike to mark or name a place by
So as to say for certain I was here
Or somewhere else: I was just far from home.
A small bird flew before me. He was careful
To put a tree between us when he lighted,
And say no word to tell me who he was
Who was so foolish as to think what he thought.
He thought that I was after him for a feather --
The white one in his tail; like one who takes
Everything said as personal to himself.
One flight out sideways would have undeceived him.
And then there was a pile of wood for which
I forgot him and let his little fear
Carry him off the way I might have gone,
Without so much as wishing him good-night.
He went behind it to make his last stand.
It was a cord of maple, cut and split
And piled -- and measured, four by four by eight.
And not another like it could I see.
No runner tracks in this year's snow looped near it.
And it was older sure than this year's cutting,
Or even last year's or the year's before.

The wood was gray and the bark warping off it
And the pile somewhat sunken. Clematis
Had wound strings round and round it like a bundle.
What held it though on one side was a tree
Still growing, and on one a stake and prop,
These latter about to fall. I thought that only
Someone who lived in turning to fresh tasks
Could so forget his handiwork on which
He spent himself, the labor of his ax,
And leave it there far from a useful fireplace
To warm the frozen swamp as best it could
With the slow smokeless burning of decay.

The Lockless Door

It went many years,
But at last came a knock,
And I thought of the door
With no lock to lock.

I blew out the light,
I tip-toed the floor,
And raised both hands
In prayer to the door.

But the knock came again
My window was wide;
I climbed on the sill
And descended outside.

Back over the sill
I bade a "Come in"
To whoever the knock
At the door may have been.

So at a knock
I emptied my cage
To hide in the world
And alter with age.

Provide, Provide

The witch that came (the withered hag)
To wash the steps with pail and rag
Was once the beauty Abishag,
The picture pride of Hollywood.
Too many fall from great and good
For you to doubt the likelihood.

Die early and avoid the fate.
Or if predestined to die late,
Make up your mind to die in state.

Make the whole stock exchange your own!
If need be occupy a throne,
Where nobody can call you crone.

Some have relied on what they knew,
Others on being simply true.
What worked for them might work for you.

No memory of having starred
Atones for later disregard
Or keeps the end from being hard.

Better to go down dignified
With boughten friendship at your side
Than none at all. Provide, provide!

To The Thawing Wind

Come with rain. O loud Southwester!
Bring the singer, bring the nester;
Give the buried flower a dream;
Make the settled snowbank steam;
Find the brown beneath the white;
But whate'er you do tonight,
Bath my window, make it flow,
Melt it as the ice will go;
Melt the glass and leave the sticks
Like a hermit's crucifix;
Burst into my narrow stall;
Swing the picture on the wall;
Run the rattling pages o'er;
Scatter poems on the floor;
Turn the poet out of door.

The Telephone

'When I was just as far as I could walk From here today, There was an hour All still When leaning with my head again a flower I heard you talk. Don't say I didn't, for I heard you say-- You spoke from that flower on the window sill- Do you remember what it was you said?' 'First tell me what it was you thought you heard.' 'Having found the flower and driven a bee away, I leaned on my head And holding by the stalk, I listened and I thought I caught the word-- What was it? Did you call me by my name? Or did you say-- Someone said "Come" -- I heard it as I bowed.' 'I may have thought as much, but not aloud.' "Well, so I came.'

The Armful

For every parcel I stoop down to seize
I lose some other off my arms and knees,
And the whole pile is slipping, bottles, buns --
Extremes too hard to comprehend at once,
Yet nothing I should care to leave behind.
With all I have to hold with hand and mind
And heart, if need be, I will do my best
To keep their building balanced at my breast.
I crouch down to prevent them as they fall;
Then sit down in the middle of them all.
I had to drop the armful in the road
And try to stack them in a better load.

Love And A Question

A stranger came to the door at eve,
And he spoke the bridegroom fair.
He bore a green-white stick in his hand,
And, for all burden, care.
He asked with the eyes more than the lips
For a shelter for the night,
And he turned and looked at the road afar
Without a window light.

The bridegroom came forth into the porch
With, 'Let us look at the sky,
And question what of the night to be,
Stranger, you and I.'
The woodbine leaves littered the yard,
The woodbine berries were blue,
Autumn, yes, winter was in the wind;
'Stranger, I wish I knew.'

Within, the bride in the dusk alone
Bent over the open fire,
Her face rose-red with the glowing coal
And the thought of the heart's desire.

The bridegroom looked at the weary road,
Yet saw but her within,
And wished her heart in a case of gold
And pinned with a silver pin.
The bridegroom thought it little to give
A dole of bread, a purse,

A heartfelt prayer for the poor of God,
  Or for the rich a curse;

But whether or not a man was asked
  To mar the love of two
By harboring woe in the bridal house,
  The bridegroom wished he knew.

Canis Major

The great Overdog
That heavenly beast
With a star in one eye
Gives a leap in the east.
He dances upright
All the way to the west
And never once drops
On his forefeet to rest.
I'm a poor underdog,
But to-night I will bark
With the great Overdog
That romps through the dark.

Blueberries

'You ought to have seen what I saw on my way To the village, through Mortenson's pasture to-day: Blueberries as big as the end of your thumb, Real sky-blue, and heavy, and ready to drum In the cavernous pail of the first one to come! And all ripe together, not some of them green And some of them ripe! You ought to have seen! ' 'I don't know what part of the pasture you mean.' 'You know where they cut off the woods—let me see— It was two years ago—or no! —can it be No longer than that? —and the following fall The fire ran and burned it all up but the wall.' 'Why, there hasn't been time for the bushes to grow. That's always the way with the blueberries, though: There may not have been the ghost of a sign Of them anywhere under the shade of the pine, But get the pine out of the way, you may burn The pasture all over until not a fern Or grass-blade is left, not to mention a stick, And presto, they're up all around you as thick And hard to explain as a conjuror's trick.' 'It must be on charcoal they fatten their fruit. I taste in them sometimes the flavour of soot. And after all really they're ebony skinned: The blue's but a mist from the breath of the wind, A tarnish that goes at a touch of the hand, And less than the tan with which pickers are tanned.' 'Does Mortenson know what he has, do you think? ' 'He may and not care and so leave the chewink To gather them for him—you know what he is. He won't make the fact that they're rightfully his An excuse for keeping us other folk out.' 'I wonder you didn't see Loren about.' 'The best of it was that I did. Do you know, I was just getting through what the field had to show And over the wall and into the road, When who should come by, with a democrat-load Of all the young chattering Lorens alive, But

Loren, the fatherly, out for a drive.' 'He saw you, then? What did he do? Did he frown? ' 'He just kept nodding his head up and down. You know how politely he always goes by. But he thought a big thought—I could tell by his eye— Which being expressed, might be this in effect: 'I have left those there berries, I shrewdly suspect, To ripen too long. I am greatly to blame." 'He's a thriftier person than some I could name.' 'He seems to be thrifty; and hasn't he need, With the mouths of all those young Lorens to feed? He has brought them all up on wild berries, they say, Like birds. They store a great many away. They eat them the year round, and those they don't eat They sell in the store and buy shoes for their feet.' 'Who cares what they say? It's a nice way to live, Just taking what Nature is willing to give, Not forcing her hand with harrow and plow.' 'I wish you had seen his perpetual bow— And the air of the youngsters! Not one of them turned, And they looked so solemn-absurdly concerned.' 'I wish I knew half what the flock of them know Of where all the berries and other things grow, Cranberries in bogs and raspberries on top Of the boulder-strewn mountain, and when they will crop. I met them one day and each had a flower Stuck into his berries as fresh as a shower; Some strange kind—they told me it hadn't a name.' 'I've told you how once not long after we came, I almost provoked poor Loren to mirth By going to him of all people on earth To ask if he knew any fruit to be had For the picking. The rascal, he said he'd be glad To tell if he knew. But the year had been bad. There had been some berries—but those were all gone. He didn't say where they had been. He went on: 'I'm sure—I'm sure'—as polite as could be. He spoke to his wife in the door, 'Let me see, Mame, we don't know any good berrying place? ' It was all he could do to keep a straight face. 'If he thinks all the fruit that grows wild is for him, He'll find he's mistaken. See here, for a whim, We'll pick in the Mortensons' pasture this year. We'll go in the morning, that is, if it's clear, And the sun shines out warm: the vines must be wet. It's so long since I picked I almost forget How we used to pick berries: we took one look round, Then sank out of sight like trolls underground, And saw nothing more of each other, or heard, Unless when you said I was keeping a bird Away from its nest, and I said it was you. 'Well, one of us is.' For complaining it flew Around and around us. And then for a while We picked, till I feared you had wandered a mile, And I thought I had lost you. I lifted a shout Too loud for the distance you were, it turned out, For when you made answer, your voice was as low As talking—you stood up beside me, you know.' 'We sha'n't have the place to ourselves to enjoy— Not likely, when all the young Lorens deploy. They'll be there to-morrow, or even to-night. They won't be too friendly—they may be polite— To people they look on as having no right To pick where they're picking. But we won't complain. You ought to have seen how it looked in the rain, The fruit mixed with water in layers of leaves, Like two kinds of jewels, a vision for thieves.'

Rose Pogonias

A saturated meadow,
Sun-shaped and jewel-small,
A circle scarcely wider
Than the trees around were tall;
Where winds were quite excluded,
And the air was stifling sweet
With the breath of many flowers, --
A temple of the heat.

There we bowed us in the burning,
As the sun's right worship is,
To pick where none could miss them
A thousand orchises;
For though the grass was scattered,
yet every second spear
Seemed tipped with wings of color,
That tinged the atmosphere.

We raised a simple prayer
Before we left the spot,
That in the general mowing
That place might be forgot;
Or if not all so favored,
Obtain such grace of hours,
that none should mow the grass there
While so confused with flowers.

Fragmentary Blue

Why make so much of fragmentary blue
In here and there a bird, or butterfly,
Or flower, or wearing-stone, or open eye,
When heaven presents in sheets the solid hue?

Since earth is earth, perhaps, not heaven (as yet)--
Though some savants make earth include the sky;
And blue so far above us comes so high,
It only gives our wish for blue a whet.

In A Disused Graveyard

The living come with grassy tread
To read the gravestones on the hill;
The graveyard draws the living still,
But never anymore the dead.
The verses in it say and say:
"The ones who living come today
To read the stones and go away
Tomorrow dead will come to stay."
So sure of death the marbles rhyme,
Yet can't help marking all the time
How no one dead will seem to come.
What is it men are shrinking from?
It would be easy to be clever
And tell the stones: Men hate to die
And have stopped dying now forever.
I think they would believe the lie.

Storm Fear

When the wind works against us in the dark,
And pelts with snow
The lowest chamber window on the east,
And whispers with a sort of stifled bark,
The beast,
'Come out! Come out!'-
It costs no inward struggle not to go,
Ah, no!
I count our strength,
Two and a child,
Those of us not asleep subdued to mark
How the cold creeps as the fire dies at length,-
How drifts are piled,
Dooryard and road ungraded,
Till even the comforting barn grows far away
And my heart owns a doubt
Whether 'tis in us to arise with day
And save ourselves unaided.

In Hardwood Groves

The same leaves over and over again!
They fall from giving shade above
To make one texture of faded brown
And fit the earth like a leather glove.

Before the leaves can mount again
To fill the trees with another shade,
They must go down past things coming up.
They must go down into the dark decayed.

They must be pierced by flowers and put
Beneath the feet of dancing flowers.
However it is in some other world
I know that this is way in ours.

The Star Splitter

`You know Orion always comes up sideways.
Throwing a leg up over our fence of mountains,
And rising on his hands, he looks in on me
Busy outdoors by lantern-light with something

I should have done by daylight, and indeed,
After the ground is frozen, I should have done
Before it froze, and a gust flings a handful
Of waste leaves at my smoky lantern chimney
To make fun of my way of doing things,
Or else fun of Orion's having caught me.
Has a man, I should like to ask, no rights
These forces are obliged to pay respect to?'
So Brad McLaughlin mingled reckless talk
Of heavenly stars with hugger-mugger farming,
Till having failed at hugger-mugger farming
He burned his house down for the fire insurance
And spent the proceeds on a telescope
To satisfy a lifelong curiosity
About our place among the infinities.

`What do you want with one of those blame things?'
I asked him well beforehand. `Don't you get one!'

`Don't call it blamed; there isn't anything
More blameless in the sense of being less
A weapon in our human fight,' he said.
`I'll have one if I sell my farm to buy it.'
There where he moved the rocks to plow the ground

And plowed between the rocks he couldn't move,
Few farms changed hands; so rather than spend years
Trying to sell his farm and then not selling,
He burned his house down for the fire insurance
And bought the telescope with what it came to.
He had been heard to say by several:
`The best thing that we're put here for's to see;
The strongest thing that's given us to see with's
A telescope. Someone in every town
Seems to me owes it to the town to keep one.
In Littleton it might as well be me.'
After such loose talk it was no surprise
When he did what he did and burned his house down.

Mean laughter went about the town that day
To let him know we weren't the least imposed on,
And he could wait---we'd see to him tomorrow.
But the first thing next morning we reflected
If one by one we counted people out
For the least sin, it wouldn't take us long
To get so we had no one left to live with.
For to be social is to be forgiving.
Our thief, the one who does our stealing from us,
We don't cut off from coming to church suppers,
But what we miss we go to him and ask for.
He promptly gives it back, that is if still
Uneaten, unworn out, or undisposed of.
It wouldn't do to be too hard on Brad
About his telescope. Beyond the age
Of being given one for Christmas gift,
He had to take the best way he knew how
To find himself in one. Well, all we said was
He took a strange thing to be roguish over.
Some sympathy was wasted on the house,

A good old-timer dating back along;
But a house isn't sentient; the house
Didn't feel anything. And if it did,
Why not regard it as a sacrifice,
And an old-fashioned sacrifice by fire,
Instead of a new-fashioned one at auction?

Out of a house and so out of a farm
At one stroke (of a match), Brad had to turn
To earn a living on the Concord railroad,
As under-ticket-agent at a station
Where his job, when he wasn't selling tickets,
Was setting out, up track and down, not plants
As on a farm, but planets, evening stars
That varied in their hue from red to green.

He got a good glass for six hundred dollars.
His new job gave him leisure for stargazing.
Often he bid me come and have a look
Up the brass barrel, velvet black inside,
At a star quaking in the other end.
I recollect a night of broken clouds
And underfoot snow melted down to ice,
And melting further in the wind to mud.
Bradford and I had out the telescope.
We spread our two legs as we spread its three,
Pointed our thoughts the way we pointed it,
And standing at our leisure till the day broke,
Said some of the best things we ever said.
That telescope was christened the Star-Splitter,
Because it didn't do a thing but split
A star in two or three, the way you split
A globule of quicksilver in your hand
With one stroke of your finger in the middle.

It's a star-splitter if there ever was one,
And ought to do some good if splitting stars
'Sa thing to be compared with splitting wood.

We've looked and looked, but after all where are we?
Do we know any better where we are,
And how it stands between the night tonight
And a man with a smoky lantern chimney?
How different from the way it ever stood?

Reluctance

Out through the fields and the woods
And over the walls I have wended;
I have climbed the hills of view
And looked at the world, and descended;
I have come by the highway home,
And lo, it is ended.

The leaves are all dead on the ground,
Save those that the oak is keeping
To ravel them one by one
And let them go scraping and creeping
Out over the crusted snow,
When others are sleeping.

And the dead leaves lie huddled and still,
No longer blown hither and thither;
The last lone aster is gone;
The flowers of the witch hazel wither;
The heart is still aching to seek,
But the feet question 'Whither?'

Ah, when to the heart of man
Was it ever less than a treason
To go with the drift of things,
To yield with a grace to reason,
And bow and accept the end
Of a love or a season?

To Earthward

Love at the lips was touch
As sweet as I could bear;
And once that seemed too much;
I lived on air

That crossed me from sweet things,
The flow of - was it musk
From hidden grapevine springs
Down hill at dusk?

I had the swirl and ache
From sprays of honeysuckle
That when they're gathered shake
Dew on the knuckle.

I craved strong sweets, but those
Seemed strong when I was young;
The petal of the rose
It was that stung.

Now no joy but lacks salt
That is not dashed with pain
And weariness and fault;
I crave the stain

Of tears, the aftermark
Of almost too much love,
The sweet of bitter bark
And burning clove.

When stiff and sore and scarred
I take away my hand
From leaning on it hard
In grass and sand,

The hurt is not enough:
I long for weight and strength
To feel the earth as rough
To all my length.

Wind And Window Flower

Lovers, forget your love,
And list to the love of these,
She a window flower,
And he a winter breeze.

When the frosty window veil
Was melted down at noon,
And the cagèd yellow bird
Hung over her in tune,
He marked her through the pane,
He could not help but mark,
And only passed her by,
To come again at dark.
He was a winter wind,
Concerned with ice and snow,
Dead weeds and unmated birds,
And little of love could know.
But he sighed upon the sill,
He gave the sash a shake,
As witness all within
Who lay that night awake.
Perchance he half prevailed
To win her for the flight
From the firelit looking-glass
And warm stove-window light.
But the flower leaned aside
And thought of naught to say,
And morning found the breeze

A hundred miles away.

The Cow In Apple-Time

Something inspires the only cow of late
To make no more of a wall than an open gate,
And think no more of wall-builders than fools.
Her face is flecked with pomace and she drools
A cider syrup. Having tasted fruit,
She scorns a pasture withering to the root.
She runs from tree to tree where lie and sweeten.
The windfalls spiked with stubble and worm-eaten.
She leaves them bitten when she has to fly.
She bellows on a knoll against the sky.
Her udder shrivels and the milk goes dry.

Love And A Question

A stranger came to the door at eve,
And he spoke the bridegroom fair.
He bore a green-white stick in his hand,
And, for all burden, care.
He asked with the eyes more than the lips
For a shelter for the night,
And he turned and looked at the road afar
Without a window light.

The bridegroom came forth into the porch
With, 'Let us look at the sky,
And question what of the night to be,
Stranger, you and I.'
The woodbine leaves littered the yard,
The woodbine berries were blue,
Autumn, yes, winter was in the wind;
'Stranger, I wish I knew.'

Within, the bride in the dusk alone
Bent over the open fire,
Her face rose-red with the glowing coal
And the thought of the heart's desire.

The bridegroom looked at the weary road,
Yet saw but her within,
And wished her heart in a case of gold
And pinned with a silver pin.

The bridegroom thought it little to give

A dole of bread, a purse,
A heartfelt prayer for the poor of God,
Or for the rich a curse;

But whether or not a man was asked
To mar the love of two
By harboring woe in the bridal house,
The bridegroom wished he knew.

The Bear

The bear puts both arms around the tree above her
And draws it down as if it were a lover
And its chokecherries lips to kiss good-by,
Then lets it snap back upright in the sky.

Her next step rocks a boulder on the wall
(She's making her cross-country in the fall).
Her great weight creaks the barbed wire in its staples
As she flings over and off down through the maples,
Leaving on one wire tooth a lock of hair.
Such is the uncaged progress of the bear.
The world has room to make a bear feel free;
The universe seems cramped to you and me.
Man acts more like the poor bear in a cage,
That all day fights a nervous inward rage,
His mood rejecting all his mind suggests.
He paces back and forth and never rests
The me-nail click and shuffle of his feet,
The telescope at one end of his beat,
And at the other end the microscope,
Two instruments of nearly equal hope,
And in conjunction giving quite a spread.
Or if he rests from scientific tread,
'Tis only to sit back and sway his head
Through ninety-odd degrees of arc, it seems,
Between two metaphysical extremes.
He sits back on his fundamental butt
With lifted snout and eyes (if any) shut
(He almost looks religious but he's not),

And back and forth he sways from cheek to cheek,
At one extreme agreeing with one Greek
At the other agreeing with another Greek
Which may be thought, but only so to speak.
A baggy figure, equally pathetic
When sedentary and when peripatetic.

In A Vale

When I was young, we dwelt in a vale
By a misty fen that rang all night,
And thus it was the maidens pale
I knew so well, whose garments trail

Across the reeds to a window light.
The fen had every kind of bloom,
And for every kind there was a face,
And a voice that has sounded in my room
Across the sill from the outer gloom.
Each came singly unto her place,
But all came every night with the mist;
And often they brought so much to say
Of things of moment to which, they wist,
One so lonely was fain to list,
That the stars were almost faded away
Before the last went, heavy with dew,
Back to the place from which she came-
Where the bird was before it flew,
Where the flower was before it grew,
Where bird and flower were one and the same.
And thus it is I know so well
Why the flower has odor, the bird has song.
You have only to ask me, and I can tell.
No, not vainly there did I dwell,
Nor vainly listen all the night long.

In Neglect

They leave us so to the way we took, As two in whom them were proved mistaken, That we sit sometimes in the wayside nook, With michievous, vagrant, seraphic look, And try if we cannot feel forsaken.

Spoils Of The Dead

Two fairies it was
On a still summer day
Came forth in the woods
With the flowers to play.

The flowers they plucked
They cast on the ground
For others, and those
For still others they found.
Flower-guided it was
That they came as they ran
On something that lay
In the shape of a man.
The snow must have made
The feathery bed
When this one fell
On the sleep of the dead.
But the snow was gone
A long time ago,
And the body he wore
Nigh gone with the snow.
The fairies drew near
And keenly espied
A ring on his hand
And a chain at his side.
They knelt in the leaves
And eerily played
With the glittering things,
And were not afraid.

And when they went home
To hide in their burrow,
They took them along
To play with to-morrow.
When you came on death,
Did you not come flower-guided
Like the elves in the wood?
I remember that I did.
But I recognised death
With sorrow and dread,
And I hated and hate
The spoils of the dead.

Hyla Brook

By June our brook's run out of song and speed.
Sought for much after that, it will be found
Either to have gone groping underground
(And taken with it all the Hyla breed
That shouted in the mist a month ago,
Like ghost of sleigh-bells in a ghost of snow)--
Or flourished and come up in jewel-weed,
Weak foliage that is blown upon and bent
Even against the way its waters went.
Its bed is left a faded paper sheet
Of dead leaves stuck together by the heat--
A brook to none but who remember long.
This as it will be seen is other far
Than with brooks taken otherwhere in song.
We love the things we love for what they are.

They Were Welcome To Their Belief

Grief may have thought it was grief.
Care may have thought it was care.
They were welcome to their belief,
The overimportant pair.

No, it took all the snows that clung
To the low roof over his bed,
Beginning when he was young,
To induce the one snow on his head.

But whenever the roof camme white
The head in the dark below
Was a shade less the color of night,
A shade more the color of snow.

Grief may have thought it was grief.
Care may have thought it was care.
But neither one was the thief
Of his raven color of hair.

Quandary

Never have I been glad or sad
That there was such a thing as bad.
There had to be, I understood,
For there to have been any good.

It was by having been contrasted
That good and bad so long had lasted.
That's why discrimination reigns.
That's why we need a lot of brains
If only to discriminate
'Twixt what to love and what to hate.
To quote the oracle at Delphi,
Love thy neighbor as thyself, aye,
And hate him as thyself thou hatest.
There quandary is at its greatest.
We learned from the forbidden fruit
For brains there is no substitute.
'Unless it's sweetbreads, ' you suggest
With innuendo I detest.
You drive me to confess in ink:
Once I was fool enough to think
That brains and sweetbreads were the same,
Till I was caught and put to shame,
First by a butcher, then a cook,
Then by a scientific book.
But ' twas by making sweetbreads do
I passed with such a high I.Q.

The Oven Bird

There is a singer eveyone has heard,
Loud, a mid-summer and a mid-wood bird,
Who makes the solid tree trunks sound again.
He says that leaves are old and that for flowers
Mid-summer is to spring as one to ten.
He says the early petal-fall is past,
When pear and cherry bloom went down in showers
On sunny days a moment overcast;
And comes that other fall we name the fall.
He says the highway dust is over all.
The bird would cease and be as other birds
But that he knows in singing not to sing.
The question that he frames in all but words
Is what to make of a diminished thing.

The Witch of Coös

I staid the night for shelter at a farm
Behind the mountains, with a mother and son,
Two old-believers. They did all the talking.

MOTHER Folks think a witch who has familiar spirits
She could call up to pass a winter evening,
But won't, should be burned at the stake or something.
Summoning spirits isn't 'Button, button,
Who's got the button,' I would have them know.

SON: Mother can make a common table rear
And kick with two legs like an army mule.

MOTHER: And when I've done it, what good have I
done?
Rather than tip a table for you, let me
Tell you what Ralle the Sioux Control once told me.
He said the dead had souls, but when I asked him
How could that be - I thought the dead were souls,
He broke my trance. Don't that make you suspicious
That there's something the dead are keeping back?
Yes, there's something the dead are keeping back.

SON: You wouldn't want to tell him what we have
Up attic, mother?

MOTHER: Bones - a skeleton.

SON: But the headboard of mother's bed is pushed

Against the' attic door: the door is nailed.
It's harmless. Mother hears it in the night
Halting perplexed behind the barrier
Of door and headboard. Where it wants to get
Is back into the cellar where it came from.

MOTHER: We'll never let them, will we, son! We'll
never !

SON: It left the cellar forty years ago
And carried itself like a pile of dishes
Up one flight from the cellar to the kitchen,
Another from the kitchen to the bedroom,
Another from the bedroom to the attic,
Right past both father and mother, and neither stopped
it.
Father had gone upstairs; mother was downstairs.
I was a baby: I don't know where I was.

MOTHER: The only fault my husband found with me -
I went to sleep before I went to bed,
Especially in winter when the bed
Might just as well be ice and the clothes snow.
The night the bones came up the cellar-stairs
Toffile had gone to bed alone and left me,
But left an open door to cool the room off
So as to sort of turn me out of it.
I was just coming to myself enough
To wonder where the cold was coming from,
When I heard Toffile upstairs in the bedroom
And thought I heard him downstairs in the cellar.
The board we had laid down to walk dry-shod on
When there was water in the cellar in spring
Struck the hard cellar bottom. And then someone

Began the stairs, two footsteps for each step,
The way a man with one leg and a crutch,
Or a little child, comes up. It wasn't Toffile:
It wasn't anyone who could be there.
The bulkhead double-doors were double-locked
And swollen tight and buried under snow.
The cellar windows were banked up with sawdust
And swollen tight and buried under snow.
It was the bones. I knew them - and good reason.
My first impulse was to get to the knob
And hold the door. But the bones didn't try
The door; they halted helpless on the landing,
Waiting for things to happen in their favour.'
The faintest restless rustling ran all through them.
I never could have done the thing I did
If the wish hadn't been too strong in me
To see how they were mounted for this walk.
I had a vision of them put together
Not like a man, but like a chandelier.
So suddenly I flung the door wide on him.
A moment he stood balancing with emotion,
And all but lost himself. (A tongue of fire
Flashed out and licked along his upper teeth.
Smoke rolled inside the sockets of his eyes.)
Then he came at me with one hand outstretched,
The way he did in life once; but this time
I struck the hand off brittle on the floor,
And fell back from him on the floor myself.
The finger-pieces slid in all directions.
(Where did I see one of those pieces lately?
Hand me my button-box- it must be there.)
I sat up on the floor and shouted, 'Toffile,
It's coming up to you.' It had its choice
Of the door to the cellar or the hall.

It took the hall door for the novelty,
And set off briskly for so slow a thing,
Stillgoing every which way in the joints, though,
So that it looked like lightning or a scribble,
>From the slap I had just now given its hand.
I listened till it almost climbed the stairs
>From the hall to the only finished bedroom,
Before I got up to do anything;
Then ran and shouted, 'Shut the bedroom door,
Toffile, for my sake!' 'Company?' he said,
'Don't make me get up; I'm too warm in bed.'
So lying forward weakly on the handrail
I pushed myself upstairs, and in the light
(The kitchen had been dark) I had to own
I could see nothing. 'Toffile, I don't see it.
It's with us in the room though. It's the bones.'
'What bones?' 'The cellar bones- out of the grave.'
That made him throw his bare legs out of bed
And sit up by me and take hold of me.
I wanted to put out the light and see
If I could see it, or else mow the room,
With our arms at the level of our knees,
And bring the chalk-pile down. 'I'll tell you what-
It's looking for another door to try.
The uncommonly deep snow has made him think
Of his old song, The Wild Colonial Boy,
He always used to sing along the tote-road.
He's after an open door to get out-doors.
Let's trap him with an open door up attic.'
Toffile agreed to that, and sure enough,
Almost the moment he was given an opening,
The steps began to climb the attic stairs.
I heard them. Toffile didn't seem to hear them.
'Quick !' I slammed to the door and held the knob.

'Toffile, get nails.' I made him nail the door shut,
And push the headboard of the bed against it.
Then we asked was there anything
Up attic that we'd ever want again.
The attic was less to us than the cellar.
If the bones liked the attic, let them have it.
Let them stay in the attic. When they sometimes
Come down the stairs at night and stand perplexed
Behind the door and headboard of the bed,
Brushing their chalky skull with chalky fingers,
With sounds like the dry rattling of a shutter,
That's what I sit up in the dark to say-
To no one any more since Toffile died.
Let them stay in the attic since they went there.
I promised Toffile to be cruel to them
For helping them be cruel once to him.

SON: We think they had a grave down in the cellar.

MOTHER: We know they had a grave down in the cellar.

SON: We never could find out whose bones they were.

MOTHER: Yes, we could too, son. Tell the truth for once.
They were a man's his father killed for me.
I mean a man he killed instead of me.
The least I could do was to help dig their grave.
We were about it one night in the cellar.
Son knows the story: but 'twas not for him
To tell the truth, suppose the time had come.
Son looks surprised to see me end a lie
We'd kept all these years between ourselves
So as to have it ready for outsiders.
But to-night I don't care enough to lie-

I don't remember why I ever cared.
Toffile, if he were here, I don't believe
Could tell you why he ever cared himself-

She hadn't found the finger-bone she wanted
Among the buttons poured out in her lap.
I verified the name next morning: Toffile.
The rural letter-box said Toffile Lajway.

The Tuft Of Flowers

I went to turn the grass once after one
Who mowed it in the dew before the sun.

The dew was gone that made his blade so keen

Before I came to view the levelled scene.

I looked for him behind an isle of trees;
I listened for his whetstone on the breeze.

But he had gone his way, the grass all mown,
And I must be, as he had been,—alone,

'As all must be,' I said within my heart,
'Whether they work together or apart.'

But as I said it, swift there passed me by
On noiseless wing a bewildered butterfly,

Seeking with memories grown dim over night
Some resting flower of yesterday's delight.

And once I marked his flight go round and round,
As where some flower lay withering on the ground.
And then he flew as far as eye could see,
And then on tremulous wing came back to me.

I thought of questions that have no reply,
And would have turned to toss the grass to dry;

But he turned first, and led my eye to look
At a tall tuft of flowers beside a brook,

A leaping tongue of bloom the scythe had spared
Beside a reedy brook the scythe had bared.

I left my place to know them by their name,
Finding them butterfly-weed when I came.

The mower in the dew had loved them thus,
By leaving them to flourish, not for us,

Nor yet to draw one thought of ours to him,
But from sheer morning gladness at the brim.

The butterfly and I had lit upon,
Nevertheless, a message from the dawn,

That made me hear the wakening birds around,
And hear his long scythe whispering to the ground,

And feel a spirit kindred to my own;
So that henceforth I worked no more alone;

But glad with him, I worked as with his aid,
And weary, sought at noon with him the shade;

And dreaming, as it were, held brotherly speech
With one whose thought I had not hoped to reach.

'Men work together,' I told him from the heart,
'Whether they work together or apart.'

Departmental

An ant on the tablecloth
Ran into a dormant moth
Of many times his size.
He showed not the least surprise.

His business wasn't with such.
He gave it scarcely a touch,
And was off on his duty run.
Yet if he encountered one
Of the hive's enquiry squad
Whose work is to find out God
And the nature of time and space,
He would put him onto the case.
Ants are a curious race;
One crossing with hurried tread
The body of one of their dead
Isn't given a moment's arrest-
Seems not even impressed.
But he no doubt reports to any
With whom he crosses antennae,
And they no doubt report
To the higher-up at court.
Then word goes forth in Formic:
'Death's come to Jerry McCormic,
Our selfless forager Jerry.
Will the special Janizary
Whose office it is to bury
The dead of the commissary

Go bring him home to his people.
Lay him in state on a sepal.
Wrap him for shroud in a petal.
Embalm him with ichor of nettle.
This is the word of your Queen.'
And presently on the scene
Appears a solemn mortician;
And taking formal position,
With feelers calmly atwiddle,
Seizes the dead by the middle,
And heaving him high in air,
Carries him out of there.
No one stands round to stare.
It is nobody else's affair
It couldn't be called ungentle
But how thoroughly departmental

Meeting And Passing

As I went down the hill along the wall
There was a gate I had leaned at for the view
And had just turned from when I first saw you
As you came up the hill. We met. But all
We did that day was mingle great and small
Footprints in summer dust as if we drew
The figure of our being less than two
But more than one as yet. Your parasol
Pointed the decimal off with one deep thrust.
And all the time we talked you seemed to see
Something down there to smile at in the dust.
(Oh, it was without prejudice to me!)
Afterward I went past what you had passed
Before we met and you what I had passed.

To E.T.

I slumbered with your poems on my breast
Spread open as I dropped them half-read through
Like dove wings on a figure on a tomb
To see, if in a dream they brought of you,

I might not have the chance I missed in life
Through some delay, and call you to your face
First soldier, and then poet, and then both,
Who died a soldier-poet of your race.

I meant, you meant, that nothing should remain
Unsaid between us, brother, and this remained--
And one thing more that was not then to say:
The Victory for what it lost and gained.

You went to meet the shell's embrace of fire
On Vimy Ridge; and when you fell that day
The war seemed over more for you than me,
But now for me than you--the other way.

How over, though, for even me who knew
The foe thrust back unsafe beyond the Rhine,
If I was not to speak of it to you
And see you pleased once more with words of mine?

The Exposed Nest

You were forever finding some new play.
So when I saw you down on hands and knees
I the meadow, busy with the new-cut hay,
Trying, I thought, to set it up on end,

I went to show you how to make it stay,
If that was your idea, against the breeze,
And, if you asked me, even help pretend
To make it root again and grow afresh.
But 'twas no make-believe with you today,
Nor was the grass itself your real concern,
Though I found your hand full of wilted fern,
Steel-bright June-grass, and blackening heads of clovers.
'Twas a nest full of young birds on the ground
The cutter-bar had just gone champing over
(Miraculously without tasking flesh)
And left defenseless to the heat and light.
You wanted to restore them to their right
Of something interposed between their sight
And too much world at once--could means be found.
The way the nest-full every time we stirred
Stood up to us as to a mother-bird
Whose coming home has been too long deferred,
Made me ask would the mother-bird return
And care for them in such a change of scene
And might out meddling make her more afraid.
That was a thing we could not wait to learn.
We saw the risk we took in doing good,
But dared not spare to do the best we could

Though harm should come of it; so built the screen
You had begun, and gave them back their shade.
All this to prove we cared. Why is there then
No more to tell? We turned to other things.
I haven't any memory--have you?--
Of ever coming to the place again
To see if the birds lived the first night through,
And so at last to learn to use their wings.

Not To Keep

They sent him back to her. The letter came
Saying... And she could have him. And before
She could be sure there was no hidden ill
Under the formal writing, he was in her sight,

Living. They gave him back to her alive
How else? They are not known to send the dead
And not disfigured visibly. His face?
His hands? She had to look, and ask,
"What was it, dear?" And she had given all
And still she had all they had they the lucky!
Wasn't she glad now? Everything seemed won,
And all the rest for them permissible ease.
She had to ask, "What was it, dear?"

"Enough,"
Yet not enough. A bullet through and through,
High in the breast. Nothing but what good care
And medicine and rest, and you a week,
Can cure me of to go again." The same
Grim giving to do over for them both.
She dared no more than ask him with her eyes
How was it with him for a second trial.
And with his eyes he asked her not to ask.
They had given him back to her, but not to keep.

Range-Finding

The battle rent a cobweb diamond-strung
And cut a flower beside a ground bird's nest
Before it stained a single human breast.
The stricken flower bent double and so hung.
And still the bird revisited her young.
A butterfly its fall had dispossessed
A moment sought in air his flower of rest,
Then lightly stooped to it and fluttering clung.

On the bare upland pasture there had spread
O'ernight 'twixt mullein stalks a wheel of thread
And straining cables wet with silver dew.
A sudden passing bullet shook it dry.
The indwelling spider ran to greet the fly,
But finding nothing, sullenly withdrew.

The Vanishing Red

He is said to have been the last Red man
In Action. And the Miller is said to have laughed--
If you like to call such a sound a laugh.
But he gave no one else a laugher's license.

For he turned suddenly grave as if to say,
'Whose business,--if I take it on myself,
Whose business--but why talk round the barn?--
When it's just that I hold with getting a thing done with.'
You can't get back and see it as he saw it.
It's too long a story to go into now.
You'd have to have been there and lived it.
They you wouldn't have looked on it as just a matter
Of who began it between the two races.

Some guttural exclamation of surprise
The Red man gave in poking about the mill
Over the great big thumping shuffling millstone
Disgusted the Miller physically as coming
From one who had no right to be heard from.
'Come, John,' he said, 'you want to see the wheel-pint?'

He took him down below a cramping rafter,
And showed him, through a manhole in the floor,
The water in desperate straits like frantic fish,
Salmon and sturgeon, lashing with their tails.
The he shut down the trap door with a ring in it
That jangled even above the general noise,
And came upstairs alone--and gave that laugh,

And said something to a man with a meal-sack
That the man with the meal-sack didn't catch--then.
Oh, yes, he showed John the wheel-pit all right.

The Need Of Being Versed In Country Things

The house had gone to bring again
To the midnight sky a sunset glow.
Now the chimney was all of the house that stood,
Like a pistil after the petals go.

The barn opposed across the way,
That would have joined the house in flame
Had it been the will of the wind, was left
To bear forsaken the place's name.

No more it opened with all one end
For teams that came by the stony road
To drum on the floor with scurrying hoofs
And brush the mow with the summer load.

The birds that came to it through the air
At broken windows flew out and in,
Their murmur more like the sigh we sigh
From too much dwelling on what has been.

Yet for them the lilac renewed its leaf,
And the aged elm, though touched with fire;
And the dry pump flung up an awkward arm;
And the fence post carried a strand of wire.

For them there was really nothing sad.

But though they rejoiced in the nest they kept,
One had to be versed in country things
Not to believe the phoebes wept.

Putting In The Seed

You come to fetch me from my work to-night
When supper's on the table, and we'll see
If I can leave off burying the white
Soft petals fallen from the apple tree
(Soft petals, yes, but not so barren quite,
Mingled with these, smooth bean and wrinkled pea);
And go along with you ere you lose sight
Of what you came for and become like me,
Slave to a Springtime passion for the earth.
How Love burns through the Putting in the Seed
On through the watching for that early birth
When, just as the soil tarnishes with weed,
The sturdy seedling with arched body comes
Shouldering its way and shedding the earth crumbs.

The Gum-Gatherer

There overtook me and drew me in
To his down-hill, early-morning stride,
And set me five miles on my road
Better than if he had had me ride,

A man with a swinging bag for'load
And half the bag wound round his hand.
We talked like barking above the din
Of water we walked along beside.
And for my telling him where I'd been
And where I lived in mountain land
To be coming home the way I was,
He told me a little about himself.
He came from higher up in the pass
Where the grist of the new-beginning brooks
Is blocks split off the mountain mass --
And hop. eless grist enough it looks
Ever to grind to soil for grass.
(The way it is will do for moss.)
There he had built his stolen shack.
It had to be a stolen shack
Because of the fears of fire and logs
That trouble the sleep of lumber folk:
Visions of half the world burned black
And the sun shrunken yellow in smoke.
We know who when they come to town
Bring berries under the wagon seat,
Or a basket of eggs between their feet;
What this man brought in a cotton sack

Was gum, the gum of the mountain spruce.
He showed me lumps of the scented stuff
Like uncut jewels, dull and rough
It comes to market golden brown;
But turns to pink between the teeth.
I told him this is a pleasant life
To set your breast to the bark of trees
That all your days are dim beneath,
And reaching up with a little knife,
To loose the resin and take it down
And bring it to market when you please

The Demiurge's Laugh

It was far in the sameness of the wood;
I was running with joy on the Demon's trail,
Though I knew what I hunted was no true god.
It was just as the light was beginning to fail
That I suddenly heard—all I needed to hear:
It has lasted me many and many a year.

The sound was behind me instead of before,
A sleepy sound, but mocking half,
As of one who utterly couldn't care.
The Demon arose from his wallow to laugh,
Brushing the dirt from his eye as he went;
And well I knew what the Demon meant.

I shall not forget how his laugh rang out.
I felt as a fool to have been so caught,
And checked my steps to make pretence
It was something among the leaves I sought
(Though doubtful whether he stayed to see).
Thereafter I sat me against a tree.